MW00325913

REPLANTED

A MEMOIR

GEORGE MALIEKAL

Cover painting by Suma Maliekal
Cover and Interior Formatting: Edge of Water Designs, edgeofwater.com

ISBNs:
Paperback: 978-1-7368684-1-6
Ebook: 978-1-7368684-0-9
Hardcover: 978-1-7368684-2-3

To Mom and Dad

"Sometimes you have to grow up before you appreciate how you grew up"

Daniel Black

TABLE OF CONTENTS

PART I: ORIGINAL ROOTS

PREFACE

The year was 2016, and it was an unusually crisp autumn morning in Long Grove, IL. The sun was low in the sky and shining brightly as I made my way to see my parents with piping-hot coffees in hand for us all. It had been almost a month since I took my dad to the emergency room; I was surprised to see him sitting upright in his bed, reading the newspaper with a content smile on his face. Compared to how he had been, prone in bed with the pain showing clearly on his face, it was a world of difference.

He was wearing a bright, checkered flannel shirt and looking energized at the rehab facility near our home. I said my greetings. He looked up from reading his paper and mused that he would be ready to go back home in a few days.

As usual, Mom was upbeat at his side. She had been with him twenty-four hours a day for the past month at the rehab center, looking after his every need. At night, she slept on a sofa bed that the center provided. I'm sure she hadn't been sleeping much, but she still managed to look energetic and optimistic every time I visited.

That day, Dad was in a jovial mood, so I brought up stories from our early days in Chicago. He always loved talking about Chicago. This is where he landed when he first came to the US, and has called Chicago home since the early sixties.

Times were tough for an immigrant on a student visa back when he first arrived, but he always spoke affectionately of Chicago, and he tried to pass on his love of the city to his children. He certainly succeeded with me. I have realized over the years that I've also echoed my dad's fondness for Chicago to my own children. They both love going into the city whenever they can.

My dad always loved speaking with people when he was in a good mood, and that morning the conversation flowed effortlessly. He was even laughing out loud as he described details about his early days as a student and his struggles to bring the rest of the family over to start a new life in Chicago.

I thought I knew the full story, but realized there were many gaps in my understanding of exactly how it had happened. I started quizzing him on several incidents that I remembered from our transition from India to Chicago. He was eager that day to fill in the gaps as best as he could. He and Mom also confirmed many of the things I remembered. He was in such high spirits that day, I walked away thinking he really had turned the corner and would be going back home soon.

That Saturday morning would be the last day I saw my dad laughing and conversing the way I always remembered him. His health deteriorated and, three weeks later, he passed away.

I spent many sleepless hours after my dad's death thinking about him and our family as we made our way from South India to Chicago to start a new life in America. It was in one of these sleepless moments that I convinced myself that I needed to write all my memories and thoughts down, if only to share them one day with my kids.

I mentioned to my wife, Suma, and daughter, Gina, that I was thinking about writing my childhood story, and about all of the people that impacted my life both in India and my early years in Chicago. I had so many vivid memories of growing up in Chicago after emigrating from India with my family at a young age. I knew that I could lean on my mom, brothers, classmates, and relatives back in India to help me fill in the gaps in my memories. I had no say in the move that we made from India to the US, but the episodes I experienced in Chicago and the many Chicagoans that I encountered shaped my life.

Like many young children, I arrived in America at an age when I was vulnerable to outside forces and other adults; thankfully, I had the good fortune of having a caring halo of parents, mentors, and friends that I was able to learn from, which had a profound impact on the choices I've made and those I continue to make in my adult life. The lessons I learned from my experiences and the guidance that I received, both directly and indirectly, from individuals around me shaped my values, my beliefs, and the type of individual that I ultimately became.

Navigating childhood in the interior of Chicago as an Indian immigrant in the early seventies was different than the idyllic life that I'd had in our rural village in India, and it forced me to quickly adapt and assimilate to a new culture and setting. This trait has carried with me throughout my life.

As the weeks and months went by after Dad's passing, my wife and daughter continued to encourage me to write my story. I kept telling them I was unsure I was up to the task, since it would be the biggest writing challenge that I had ever taken on.

After months of just talking about it, my daughter said to me one night, "Stop talking about it and just start writing, Dad." She was right. I had a lot to say, so I decided that night I was going to take a shot at it. I was going to write the story of my youth, of the city and its people that shaped me.

I knew in my heart that the experiences I encountered in Chicago in those early years added to the molding of the individual I became. In eager preparation, I tried to look through all the old photos of our time in India and our early years in Chicago. Seeing those photos of my extended family and the friends who were part of my inner circle was the trigger that I needed.

Reflecting back on those days fifty years later, I knew I had an interesting perspective. The educational path I chose, my work career, and my other accomplishments have allowed my family and I to have a great life to date, but what defined me and set the wheels in motion were my experiences and the people that I looked to when I was a boy growing up in Chicago. I am convinced that this made me the individual I have become. Those critical years were the foundation of what I valued and the way I was going to live my life.

So here it is, as best as I can tell it.

CHAPTER 1

THE ARRIVAL

My family together with Dad in Chicago two weeks
after our arrival - December 1969

Mom shook me gently awake from my sleep and told me that we had arrived. I was exhausted from the long flight and had immediately fallen asleep on the ride from the airport. I rubbed open my eyes and, realizing we had reached our destination, jumped out of the car to see what America was all about. After almost a two-day journey from India, we had finally arrived in Chicago and the house where we were going to settle.

Standing on the footpath next to the street with my mom and two brothers, I noticed the falling white flakes and smoke that came out of our mouths. Mom saw my startled look and assured me that this was normal for Chicago in the cold season. She quickly turned away to secure my little brother, who had just turned five years old.

With my hand outstretched to catch the dancing white flakes, I played, blowing out air and delighting in how the smoke curled every which way. When I looked around, expanding my attention to take in all the exciting new things, I saw the exceptionally wide streets, peculiar houses with angular roofs, and unusually bare treetops that all appeared as if they were dusted white. They glistened like freshly-grated coconut, which my grandmother would be using for the evening meal back home.

The early evening sky was pitch-black, even though Dad had told me it was only 6PM. Looking up into the darkness, I couldn't even spot one star, but I could see the area near me somewhat clearly. The trees were devoid of leaves, and the streetlight next to us shimmered and sparkled off the fresh, crisp, white flakes sitting atop the barren, black branches. It looked as if there had been a massive fire that singed the leaves off all the trees, and now they were being coated by the white, shredded coconut flakes falling from the sky.

I tried to remember for a moment if I had ever seen a tree without leaves back in India. The mango and tamarind trees that I frequently attempted to climb or throw rocks at to get fruit from while on my way to school were always full of deep, green leaves and delicious food hanging on long stems, swaying back and forth against the bluest of skies.

That thought quickly left me as I stared up and down the street I now lived on. I couldn't fathom the unending line of cars parked on both sides of the street. Instead of living greenery, the soft earth underfoot, life, and fresh air, there were bare branches, concrete, and an eerie silence.

As my family and I stood next to the apple-red American sedan, waiting for Dad and his friend who had driven us from the airport to get all the luggage, I could make out the shapes and some detail of the neighboring houses. But in that wintry time of quiet desolation, there was no color to be seen. It was only gray and white.

Overwhelmed with the disparity of my surroundings juxtaposed with where I had been mere hours before, I looked closely to see if there was anyone in the houses. Perhaps I was hoping to see boys my age that I could play marbles with in the morning, as I was used to doing. I squinted my eyes so that I could focus on the windows, but I was disappointed to find my view being blocked by drapes.

It was strange that we were the only ones outside. There was no one walking the streets that evening or gathered near the houses as far as I could see. Back home there would be people milling all around, with adults conversing and children playing, especially in the early evening.

I wondered for a moment what my school friends there were doing. I remembered what Mom had told me about how "when it's night in America, it's daytime in India;" my friends were probably all playing marbles or tag prior to the start of classes.

At that moment I regretted not hiding my valuable stash of marbles in the suitcase. Mom had told me I could not take them with me when packing for the trip. I already missed them and the greater scope of life they had represented; I longed for my friends, but at the same time my head was full of anticipation to see our new place thousands of miles away from home. Longing and loneliness, excitement and adventure, all swirled about, while my emotional stamina was weakened from the trip itself and the shock of the change.

The wind picked up, and a cold chill ripped through my body. I had never felt that kind of chill before as we walked through an opened gate towards our new home. We stepped on to a narrow, concrete walkway that was adjacent to a two-story, boxy building that led to another smaller building situated in the rear, which was to be our new home. The path leading there was covered in white, and shone back to us in an inviting manner. This visual is forever seared into my memory: the feel of chill on the wind and that snow-covered path beckoning ... it's one of those things that hits you and stays with you.

My heart was pounding in anticipation. I was unsure about what was going to happen next, so I stayed close in front of my mom, who brought some level of safety and comfort in an otherwise stressful transition. My two younger brothers also clung close to her side as we started up the path, their own anxiousness showing in their faces, the way they held their bodies, and the way they moved; I knew we were all in the same boat, but, being the oldest, I tried to appear more confident, hoping to be an example for them.

Suitcase in hand, Dad led the way in his long black coat and a funny, oval-shaped hat. His tall white friend followed behind him, also wearing a long black coat and similar hat.

The man was friendly and had asked numerous questions, but I just told him my name and gave him my best smile because I couldn't understand a thing he was saying. I had already forgotten his strange name and resorted to calling him "uncle." He spoke English in rapid fashion to my dad while walking ahead of us. I could barely make out a few words of what Dad said, and I really did not comprehend anything his friend was saying.

I had told my mother earlier at the airport that I didn't need the ugly red sweater I was wearing, which was certainly not enough to keep out the icy chill that made me shiver. I had never worn a sweater in my life, because it was always nice and warm back home, but I was glad I had it on now. To be thrust into that icy chill, to know what a sweater felt like for the first time—it is almost incomprehensible for native Chicagoans.

My feet were tingling, and I was slipping as I tried to keep my balance. Even though it was a new and uneasy feeling, it was exhilarating to be able to slide back and forth on the slippery path to our new house. This was a welcome distraction from how cold it was that night. The white flakes falling from the sky were getting larger than before, and I could see the top of my mom's head turning white as she kept trying to wipe her face and hair with her free hand, all while carrying my youngest brother, Joseph.

Joseph's face was completely covered with my mom's scarf to keep him warm, but it looked and sounded like he was struggling mightily just to breathe. The cold air came like knives into our unaccustomed lungs, and what the young cannot understand with words they can understand with their bodies.

My brother James was hanging onto my mom's now-wet sari, mesmerized as he cautiously scanned the strange new landscape. James usually loudly complained about going to any new place, and his silence in those moments felt eerie to me, leaving me uneasy that he would be at such a loss for words as to suppress his usual personality.

Mom bent down slightly and whispered to us; she explained that it was snowing, and that this happened here often. She tried to reassure us all while trying to keep her own balance and my younger brothers on their feet.

"Snow," I muttered under my breath. I pondered what my dad had mentioned in the car as I tried to take in everything that I was experiencing in that instant in time. He had mentioned that there was a chance that it would snow heavily that evening. I didn't know exactly what that meant at the time.

As we reached the end of the path, Dad proudly announced that we were here, and he opened the front door to our new house. It looked small compared to my grandmother's house back home. By the time we had reached the end of the path, I had learned to keep better balance, and I quickly slid past Mom, Dad, my brothers, and my new American "uncle" to enter our new place. With an exaggerated first step, I took my right foot over the threshold.

That was over fifty years ago, early in the evening of December 5th, 1969, but I can still vividly recall the details of my slippery slide on the freshly-fallen Chicago snow that had covered the path leading to our first apartment. It was a tremendously rich tapestry for a first impression. Every sense was assaulted; or at least, it had felt like an assault with my fatigue and my vulnerability being as it was.

Six months earlier, Neil Armstrong had walked on the strange and unknown landscape of the moon, and as I think back to my early evening walk up the snow-covered path in December, 1969, I can understand a little how Mr. Armstrong felt; that day I stood in a strange new land. I was nine and a half years old, and my life to date had been sailing on smoothly. As I took my giant leap from Southern India to the US and entered my new home on 1019 N. Wood Street in Chicago's East Village neighborhood, I knew my future was about to be redirected to a different path.

CHAPTER 2

MY OASIS

Me and my brothers with Mom,
Puthenchira, India 1965

It was another beautiful sunny morning in the front yard of my maternal grandmother's house in Puthenchira, India. I was four and half years old standing with my grandmother and my mother's older sister, Aunt Daisy, who was holding hands with my brother James. We were at the bottom of the steps leading to the narrow dirt road by the front yard entrance. Even now, all these years later, I can still see the moss-covered, reddish brick wall on the right side of the front yard with the large banana plants elegantly arching over from the neighbor's yard.

In the early morning sun, the dew on the surface of the young, pale green bananas had started to drip at the ends, which could be seen peeking out from their opened purple flower pods. The wind picked up, and shadows from the banana leaves danced on colorful roses and hibiscus bushes with large, showy red blooms that lined the corner of the dirt yard. I can still feel the coolness of the sandy dirt on my bare feet as I fidgeted and waited.

We were all waiting anxiously for my mom to come home from the hospital. She had been gone for two or three days, and I really missed her. My aunt and grandmother stayed with my brother James and me, but, as comforting as their care was, we still missed our mom.

I heard the familiar hum of a car engine in the distance and I ran past the front entrance and onto the dirt road. The almond-colored Ambassador was just visible at the far end advancing towards the house, careening past the trees that formed a tunnel over the dirt road. As I waited in the middle of the road with a large grin planted on my face, my aunt ran up behind me and yanked me back down the steps, spilling me into the front yard just as the car screeched to a stop where I had previously stood by the main entrance.

The back door of the Ambassador opened wide and my mom, in a pure white sari, stepped out of the car with the help of my Aunt Daisy, my new little brother in hand. He was wrapped tightly in a white, linen garment and I could see two eyes peering out.

This scene is etched into my brain and forms my earliest memory. I can still see the brick wall out front dwarfing a small, black iron gate where my mom and new little brother first emerged. As I ran back up the steps by the iron gate to meet her, her face broke into the biggest smile as she cradled the baby and bent gingerly down to show me.

Flanked by the rest of the group, my mom strolled back to the house with the new baby, up the steps that led to a small veranda attached to the front of the house.

The entrance into the veranda space was separated by white, round pillars. I took a quick spin around, wrapping my outstretched right hand on the adjacent column. I was thrilled that my mom and new little brother were finally home, and I let my exuberance show for all to see.

My Grandmother Rosa's house stood tall as a traditional South Indian home built at the turn of the 20th century, with row upon row of burnt orange-colored stone tiles lining the roof. The main entryway from the sitting room opened into a central courtyard that was the heart of the living space, connecting the remaining rooms on all four sides. Separating the open courtyard from the interior rooms was a wide, partially covered walkway. The open space provided plenty of room for my brothers and I to play when it was raining or dark outside. The open space on one side also contained our dining room table where we took all our meals.

The house was nestled in a quiet area of our village, which resembled a small tropical forest. The coconut trees surrounding the back of the house reached high into the sky away from the other vegetation, seeking the open sunlight. Their green, feather-shaped leaves floated in the sky like giant, propped-up umbrellas, giving shade and watching over us. The left side of the house had a side yard enclosed by a brick wall where my brothers, cousins, friends, and I spent most of our time playing. At the end of the yard there stood a small, semi-enclosed dwelling for our cow that provided us with fresh milk in the morning.

This house, and the town of Puthenchira, was my heavenly domain during my early childhood.

The house had been in my mother's side of the family for generations. It was the house that my great-grandfather built as he was starting his family. When I was growing up, this continued to be the main house of my mom's family; after my grandfather passed away, this was where my grandmother lived for the remainder of her life. My grandfather passed away relatively young and as I was only two years old, most of my memories of him are formed from stories.

According to my mom, everyone in the village liked him because he was easygoing, generous, and always had a kind word to say. He worked for the Indian railway as a conductor and devoted the rest of his time to his family. As in most South Indian families, the main house was where family members resided until the children were married and had families of their own.

When I was living with my Grandmother Rosa, I didn't realize how difficult it must've been for her after my grandfather died. I always remember her as energetic and without any complaints, just like my mom. It probably helped her immensely that one of her daughters and three of her grandkids were able to live with her at such a difficult time. She was always caring and watched over me and my brothers.

My mother's family with my mom, Aunt Daisy, and Uncle Sunny

After my grandmother's passing in 2007, the house passed down to the oldest male in the family, which is my Uncle Sunny. He recently renovated the house so that it can be a vacation home for weekend getaways for him and his family.

On one of my visits to India after the renovation was complete, I was able to see the remodeled house. I personally thought the charm of the original house was altered, but I'm glad my uncle made the needed renovations so that the house could continue to stand. It can be tricky to retain the charm of the past while updating for the present, and I know my perceptions are heavily skewed by such strong memories of growing up there.

My grandmother's house is of great significance to me, not only because I spent my early childhood there, but also because, as I came to understand from my mom, this was the house where I was born. Unlike my brothers, who were born in hospitals, I was delivered by a midwife. The room I was born in remains unaltered, and I show my children every time we visit where their dad came into the world. It is currently being used as a food storage room.

The room and the house could be famous in the future, because it is also the house where my grandfather's brother's son was born. He grew up to be a priest and eventually became the Bishop of the nearby town of Irinjalakuda. He made many meaningful contributions to his flock, and for the greater community, regardless of their religion. There has been local talk recently that he could be up for sainthood one day. If he does become a saint, then the house and room that he and I were born in could become a shrine and would probably be never torn down. I've only met the Bishop on a few occasions, but I would be thrilled if the house continued to stand.

Puthenchira is a rural village in the southern state of Kerala, which is in the southern tip of India on the western coast. Kerala is unique to India not only due to its many scenic waterways, lush tropical landscape, and scrumptious cuisine, but also due to its diversity of people. Kerala's proximity to the coast, and the many exotic spices that are indigenous to the area, led explorers from many parts of the world to cross oceans to explore it. The Chinese, the Dutch, and the Portuguese all landed on the tropical Malabar coastline and left their indelible mark on the people of Kerala.

Unlike the rest of India, there is also religious diversity. Hinduism is the most prominent religion in India, but in Kerala Hindus only comprise roughly half of the population, with the other half evenly split between Muslims and Christians. There are always local disputes between the various religious communities, but mostly the people live in relative harmony.

The state also boasts a strong healthcare system and has the highest literacy rate in India, with most of the children attending schools on a regular basis.

Keralites speak Malayalam, one of the many unique languages spoken in India. Puthenchira is a Christian community, and in the 1960's had a population of a few thousand people. It consisted mainly of farmers and small businesses owners providing the necessities to its citizens. The village at the time did not have electricity, telephones, or running water.

That was Puthenchira on paper: but for me as a child, it was my paradise, with the greenest rice paddy fields, the tastiest mangoes, and the tallest coconut trees reaching up to the sky everywhere. Jackfruit, multiple varieties of bananas, papayas, and cashews all grew on the land among numerous other tropical fruits that I am unable to translate.

Because Kerala is so close to the coast and just north of the equator, the climate is always warm. We only had two seasons that I could remember. There was always a short, intense rainy season and endlessly hot sunny days.

There were cars and busses on the roads of Puthenchira, but they were few and far between. My mode of transportation was either walking or riding on the bus with my mom and her sister, my Aunt Daisy. She lived in a nearby town, but she came often with my many cousins during school vacations. I always liked when Aunt Daisy was home, because she always brought us gifts, helped me with my homework, and would take us shopping.

I always looked forward to taking the bus to go on shopping excursions in the nearby towns. There were only two buses that ran through the town.

They were known to locals as the green ABT and the red Usha. They connected us to the neighboring towns where relatives lived or where there were bigger stores.

The red Usha bus was my favorite, and it shined with cranberry red walls with mustard yellow trim. In contrast, the ABT bus had dark, menacing green paint with black and white trim. I would still get on the ABT bus, but I always preferred red Usha. Buses in Kerala were open to the air, since there was no glass on the windows. The main roads were bumpy and dusty, but whenever I was on the red Usha bus with the wind in my face, I felt like I was moving as fast as a race car. Looking out, one could see tea and toddy[1] shops lining the main road, with local patrons milling around. I would find any reason to get off and visit the small side street shops so that I could get a sweet or some roasted cashews.

At that time, my mom, two brothers, and I lived with my grandma, because my dad was already in America. He had left to study at an American university in Chicago as soon as his student visa was issued. My mom was four months pregnant with my youngest brother when he left to establish a life for us on the other side of the world, and it took another agonizing four and a half years before my dad would see his youngest son for the first time.

I knew my dad was in America because my mom would tell us daily about his activities and occasionally show us photos. She would always tell us about the wonderful sights in America, and how one day we would be joining him. I didn't really pay close attention, because I had no idea what America was like. We did not have a TV, and the only glimpses of America I saw where the fuzzy backgrounds on the pictures that my dad sent. I was more worried about when my next marble game was or when I was going to meet up with my school friends.

I knew the photos my mother shared were of my dad because she told

---

1   A local alcoholic drink made from fermented coconut palm nectar.

me, but I had no memory of him growing up in India. My non-photographic memories of my dad only begin when I was nine years old, from when he made a visit to our house for a short time before returning to America.

I never thought too much about going to America because I had my mom, grandma, and my two brothers living with me, so I was never alone and I always felt safe. My grandmother also had two other people living with us in the house. My grandpa's younger brother, who was never married, lived with us, and Pilan *chettan*,[2] who helped her with all the household chores. He also managed the property and finances for her, and was considered an extension of the family.

My *Kochuappapan*[3] and Pilan *chettan* were two people that I liked very much, because they really watched over us. Since my mom and grandmother were two women living alone with three young kids in a rural village, they provided stability and security for the family.

My Uncle Sunny, who was studying to be a physician at the time, would often visit during his breaks from medical school and stay with us for long stretches of time. As my mom's younger brother, he would spend time with us and take us to many local events, but I thought he was way too strict.

During vacations, when the whole extended family on my mother's side was staying at my grandmother's home, he would always tell my brothers, my five cousins, and me that it was either time to do our school work or to take an afternoon nap at the most inopportune time. This took place usually just when we were really getting into our playtime activities. Even though he was strict with us, he always watched over us and helped fill the gap of not having my dad around for short periods of time. Thinking back, I would have probably behaved the same way if I had to babysit eight kids running around the house during my vacation.

2   The term "*chettan*," or "brother," is used with anyone who is older as a sign of respect
3   The Malayalam term for great-uncle

My grandmother Rosa's home in Puthenchira prior to the remodel

Many of my uncles and aunts on my dad's side of the family also lived in Puthenchira. They all lived on the other side of the village, in a neighborhood about a mile and a half from my grandma's house. My dad, who was the youngest, had four brothers and four sisters, so we were always visiting some relative or another.

Both my Uncle Paul and Uncle Anthony had large families, so I had many cousins that were close to my age. It was always fun sleeping over with them. Uncle Anthony's house on the western side of Puthenchira was the house my dad grew up in, and it had been in the Maliekal family for several generations. That vast property sat slightly above ground and backed into a huge rice paddy field.

During the rainy season, the entire paddy field filled with water, which was desperately needed for the rice to grow and deliver a good harvest. Due to the open fields, it was always windy by the house, especially at the water's edge. Coconut trees adjusting to the high winds leaned towards the water. One could easily climb up to the middle of the leaning tree over the water. My older cousins always did this, but I was too chicken to ever try it. I can still remember staring out into the sky during picturesque sunsets above the rice paddy fields: the coconut trees hung over the water, a few of them shaped like lounge chairs with an umbrella on top.

There was a small lagoon in the rear of the yard that captured rainwater and the overflow from the paddy fields during the rainy season. The lagoon always had plenty of fish in its belly. Surrounding the lagoon, closer to the house were an array of fruit trees with something always in season, including tropical grapefruit, cashews, pears, and my favorite, mangoes.

Every year, the lagoon was emptied using a pump so that the fish at the bottom could be captured. Workmen would then separate all the fish from the mud and take them to the town market to be sold. I always liked to watch the water being pumped out until only a small pool of muddy water was left. Various fish, eels, and sometimes what I thought were snakes could be seen swimming in the shallow water.

I would take a few steps back from the edge of the lagoon when I saw snakes, because they always sent a shiver down my spine. Snakes were common in Kerala, with many of them poisonous, and I spent a good deal of my childhood worrying about these slithery creatures biting me and injecting their lethal venom.

CHAPTER 3

"I HATE SNAKES"

King cobra

My dad's mom was religious and always encouraged her children to devote themselves to the Catholic Church, mostly as priests and nuns. As a result, the Maliekal family had two priests and three nuns. My dad was also encouraged to become a priest, but it was not something he wanted to pursue.

My favorite uncle was my Uncle Father John, who was the fourth-oldest in the Maliekal family. He would always treat me like a grown-up, and I frequently visited his parish in a nearby town called Mattom, where he served as the pastor. I would stay with him for a few days during my school vacations as his guest. Since my younger brothers had no interest in leaving Mom and Grandma, I had all the attention when I went to visit. I always liked staying with him because I slept in a nice bed instead of on the matted floor as I was used to back home, and I had western breakfasts with bread and butter.

I can still remember the first time I had bread and butter. It was warm and salty as I caressed it in my mouth for perhaps longer than strictly necessary prior to swallowing. I would eagerly look for a second helping, which my uncle always obliged.

During my stay, we met with many priests and nuns that were around the parish and visitors that came to see my uncle. We also went to church quite a bit; unsurprising considering our family and the general church-going nature of the place in that time. Despite some of the visit dragging, the great surroundings, the mouthwatering food, and talking to my uncle more than made up for this. I always had interesting conversations with Uncle Father John when I was young, and that continued on my many return visits as an adult on a wide range of topics, right up until the year he passed away.

Rev. Msgr. John Maliekal, my favorite uncle

My uncle was also the priest that presided over all our Catholic ceremonies including my baptism, first communion, and my wedding. My uncle would tell me about the priesthood and gently encouraged me to think about becoming a priest. I seriously considered doing just that when I was eight years old, because I figured I could get used to eating that type of food, sleeping in a fancy bed, and having frequent visitors, while at the same time helping people in the community. But it was a fleeting consideration because of all the sacrifices one had to make to become a Catholic priest.

Back in Puthenchira, school was about to begin again. This was when I was going into 4th grade. I was excited about going back to school, and always enjoyed being with my classmates. I especially liked walking back and forth from school with my closest classmates. I went for my elementary education at St. Mary's of Kuzhikkattussery. The school still stands to this day. While attending, it was a square, two-story complex with a large courtyard in the middle. The courtyard was used for assemblies, sports activities, and as a playground during recess.

The organized sporting activities were reserved for the upper classes, so I usually ended up playing marbles or tag in the playground during free time. I try to visit my school every time I go back to Kerala, and each time I go, there seems to be new buildings added to the complex. Seeing it again usually brings me back to memories of school mornings when I would meet my classmates near a tea shop so we could start the day together.

First, I had to walk along the side road from my grandmother's house that led up to the junction on the main road. This road was narrow and surrounded by greenery from the neighbor's yards. I always checked out the mango trees along the way to see if there were any ripe ones that I could knock down by throwing a stone, earning me a tasty fruit. I had been honing my throwing skills over the years, but occasionally one would go astray, missing the fruit. I never knew exactly where these errant throws ended up, but I did hear yelling once in a while. I usually ran quickly away, and was proud that I never once got caught.

As I walked up the road, the scariest part was the stretch just before the junction. There, it almost became a tunnel, with walls of dirt built up on both sides and the neighboring houses and surrounding land rising above. The houses were built away from this section of the road, so it was secluded. The dirt walls on the sides of this stretch contained many holes, which my older cousins warned were snake holes that I should never go near. With that, my curiosity died, and I never even peered in to inspect the holes; instead, I tried to sprint through that stretch as fast as I could so that I did not have to deal with those guys.

"I hate snakes," was a phrase I mumbled to myself often. I couldn't help but chuckle when Indiana Jones, faced with slithering reptiles on the big screen, shouted out the same phrase on *Raiders of the Lost Ark*, a movie I enjoyed many years later on its opening night in Chicago.

As soon as I got by the snake holes, my heart rate and my pace would slow, and I'd breathe easier before meeting up with my friends on the main road leading to my elementary school. On the way, we would always stop at the small street stands and stare at the large, glass candy jars filled with treats wrapped in brightly-colored foil. They twinkled in the sunlight, and the glass jars were symmetrically lined up on the counters of the small shop stalls in quite an eye-catching display. As soon as the shop merchants spotted us, we would be shooed away, as they knew we weren't going to buy anything.

We had to walk about a mile to reach the school, but the weather was usually nice, and talking and playing with my friends always made the time go by quickly.

My school was like many other Catholic schools in Kerala, with nuns teaching most of the classes. We were expected to wear uniforms, and the nuns were always strict. One of my aunts on my dad's side, Aunt Sister

Ethelred, was my second-grade teacher. Even though I really liked her, this was not always fun, because she expected a lot from me and I always felt the pressure. She was much more serious in the classroom than when I met her at family gatherings. I was straight as an arrow in school, but always envied the kids who *could* get into a little trouble.

I always hated not following the rules, and if I slipped up I felt anxious because I knew it would get back to my mom instantly. But that was mostly back in second grade; finishing up fourth grade saw me really enjoying my school. I even managed to break some rules, like showing up late for a class occasionally so that I could play marbles or tag with my friends just a little bit longer during recess. I was doing well in my classes, had many friends, and I was happy as can be.

On one of our visits to Puthenchira with my kids when they were old enough to explore the landscape, I warned them to watch for snakes and mentioned to them about the up-close encounter I had with a poisonous one. I was eight or nine years old at the time, and it was an event in my life that I could never forget. Even now, the memory sends shivers down my spine.

I was playing in the side yard of my Grandmother Rosa's house all alone when I got really hungry. I called out to Mom to see if dinner was ready.

She replied, "It is only five o'clock. It won't be ready for another couple of hours."

Not happy with that answer, I walked through the gate that led to the *luika*[4] tree at the back of the house. I looked up to see if there were any remaining ripe fruit that I could knock down using a long stick. I couldn't spot any, so to hold my hunger pains at bay I decided to run into the house and quickly get a snack from the pantry without my mom or grandma catching me.

There was construction taking place in the area, so rocks were piled

---

4   A *luika* is a tart, cherry-type fruit

up near the back fence. I made a dash for the house and, as I was about to cross the threshold of the fence, there it was, waiting for me: a huge snake, stretched out and sunbathing across the area that I was just about to step into.

My view to the entrance of the fence was slightly blocked by the rock pile, so I couldn't get a clear view of the snake; by the time I got close to the entrance, I had already built up enough momentum from my running start that I could not stop myself. I was in no man's land, and I had to somehow cross the fence by hurdling over the snake. I leaped into the air with my mouth gaping open, attempting to scream, but no sound came out. Out of the corner of my eye, I thought I saw the snake try to take a bite at my ankles, which were stretched ever-so-close to the body of the snake.

I made it over the threshold of the fence and quickly ran into the house. I looked back and saw the snake slither to the side of the yard inside the fence.

As I approached the side entrance of the house, my scream finally acquired volume, and my mom and Pilan *chettan* both came running outside.

"What's wrong?" they asked me frantically.

I pointed towards the snake, but the words coming out of my mouth were not making any sense. Finally, the word "snake" came out. I was crying and my body was still shaking, so my mom hugged me tightly.

Pilan *chettan* spotted the snake near the fence and he started going over by the side of the fence to take a closer look.

"No, don't go there! It's a cobra," I cautioned urgently.

He turned casually to reply. "Don't worry; I'll take care of it." Before I could say anything more, he was crouched down and hovering over the head of the snake with his right hand extended; he quickly grabbed the snake just below the head. He then brought his hand back and forcefully threw it against the side of the brick fence. The snake careened off the fence and landed on the ground, shivered for a few seconds, and then lay still.

Pilan *chettan* came over to my mom. "It's dead, and it's not a cobra," he said. "But it *is* poisonous. Thank God you weren't bitten."

My mom inspected my legs quickly, and was relieved that I did not have any bite marks. I was only wearing my shorts and a T shirt, and I did not have any shoes or sandals on, so I consider myself lucky. Ever since that incident, when I'm in India I rarely wear shorts: I instead bear the heat with my jeans and high-top shoes always on.

My kids had a real good laugh when I relayed this story, and my daughter Gina still recreates the incident by straddling the same fence with her mouth wide open, saying, "This is what Dad looked like!"

My daughter Gina recreating my close-up snake encounter

One of my most vivid memories of my time in Puthenchira was when my Uncle Sunny got married. I don't remember much of the wedding ceremony itself, which took place at the local church, but I clearly remember all the fun my cousins and I had at the reception. We were happy that the church ceremony had ended (after what seemed like hours), and we all came back to my grandmother's house in a car.

The reception was held at my grandmother's house, as most Puthenchira wedding receptions were held at the family home at the time. The side and front yards were enclosed with a coconut palm leaf structure for walls and a roof with aromatic jasmine garlands hanging all over the ceiling. Chairs and tables were neatly arranged for all our relatives.

I vividly remember the time because my cousins and I were completely free without anyone telling us what to do. My mom, grandma, and aunt were too busy working or talking to relatives, and my Uncle Sunny, who would usually keep us in check, was too busy with his new bride.

I'm sure I ran at least ten kilometers that day, just chasing my cousins and playing games that we made up on the spot. My brand-new black shorts and white cotton shirt that my mom had bought special for the occasion did not look that great after all the playing we did in the dirt yard, and I was not sure where exactly my brand-new black dress shoes had disappeared to. I could always run faster and cut corners quicker without my shoes, so I had probably ditched them early on. I figured I would deal with my mother on that after I had my full share of fun that day.

We also took it upon ourselves to eat and drink as much food as possible. The intoxicating aroma of the wedding version of beef and chicken curries were mouthwatering. Multiple varieties of fried fish were lined up on a table, and they made my stomach growl even louder. There were plenty of vegetable dishes laid out also, but I skipped over them every time.

The food had all been cooked onsite the previous day by a number of locally-hired chefs. I remembered on the days leading up to the wedding that large, steel pots were used to prepare the meat and fish curries behind my grandmother's house. I had begged to sample many of the dishes the evening prior to the wedding, but was told by my mom that I would have to wait for the wedding day to eat the meals prepared for the reception.

I made up for it the next day by extensively sampling all the delicious meat and fish curries. I also drank plenty of soda water to wash it all down from the bottles that lined one end of the food table. I can still see the blue marble inside the top of the old-style soda water bottles, which acted as the seal for the carbonation. This was the closest that I ever got to drinking pop in Puthenchira.

CHAPTER 4

AN AMERICAN VISITOR

My dad after completion of his Master's program at
DePaul University in Chicago - January 1968

Soon after the start of my school year in 5th grade, my mom told me
that Dad was coming to visit us. Excited to finally see the man from
the pictures, I immediately told all my friends that my dad from America
was coming, and many of them told me that he would bring gifts for us.
I tried to imagine what type of items he would bring us, because I was
not sure what kids played with in America. I had no clue, but this tidbit
only added to my anticipation.

The night that he came is one my mom and I will never forget. We did
not have any telephones in Puthenchira at the time, so the only method
to send an urgent message overseas was through telegrams. My mom

knew from letters from Dad that he was coming that week, but she did not have any of the specific details. She never received the letter he later said he had sent with all the details.

My dad had also sent a telegram to Uncle Father Callistus, his brother, with all the flight details prior to his departure. My uncle was then to communicate to my mom and arrange a pick-up at the Cochin airport so that we could all be reunited.

However, my mom never received word of any of this. According to my mom, the person who transcribed the message misspelled my dad's name, and my uncle thought it was a message for someone else when the telegraph office contacted him.

In the meantime, my Uncle Anthony, who lived on the west end of town in the original Maliekal house, was sick and had to be admitted to the hospital. My mom decided to go with my baby brother Joseph to the house for a few days to keep my aunt company and help out with her large family. My brother James and I remained at my grandma's house. My mom's brother and his new bride, Aunty Alice, were also staying there.

Therefore, circumstances were set up so that by early evening my new aunt came running into the courtyard dining area where Grandma, my uncle, my brother, and I were gathered.

She shouted excitedly at us, "Xavier *chettan* is outside in a taxi. He is outside!"

"Xavier *chettan*; how could it be him?" my Uncle Sunny replied to her in a playful and sarcastic tone.

"We didn't receive word that he was arriving tonight. And besides, you have never even seen him, so how do you even know it's him?"

"I've seen him in plenty of photos," retorted Aunty Alice. "I know his face when I see it. It's him."

After further convincing, we all finally went out front, and now Uncle Sunny was also excitedly shouting as my dad approached the house.

"It's *chettan*, it really is him."

Dad had landed in Cochin airport that afternoon and was perplexed that no one was there to meet him, leaving him greatly concerned that something had happened. Only after he managed to get a taxi on his own at the airport and saw my brother James and I did he feel relieved.

Standing on the front veranda, he peered inside the house to see where my mom and baby brother Joseph were. He became quite concerned when he couldn't see them. But, after we told him that Mom and Joseph were at Uncle Anthony's house, he calmed down and finally entered the house he had been away from for so long.

After getting a bite to eat, he wanted to set out to Uncle Anthony's house to see Mom and his youngest son, whom he had never met, as soon as possible. From the moment he came into the house, my eyes never left his figure. I wanted to remember it all. I seared everything into my mind, drinking in the return of this man who had, until then, only been a two-dimensional person confined to photographs: and not terribly good ones at that. Seeing him in person was causing my young heart and mind to do flip-flops as I processed his being, his presence, in person.

He was light-skinned, like my little brother, but had curly, jet-black hair just like me. He wore a crisp, white, short-sleeved shirt, and he had black, square-framed glasses that made him look very important. My dad was a little smaller than the towering figure that I had imagined living in America, as I am sure the mythos surrounding him could only have *been* larger than life, but I was sure happy to see him.

I told him I wanted to go along with him to see Mom. He, Pilan *chettan*, and I started our trek to Uncle Anthony's house that evening. Darkness had fallen, and Pilan *chettan* suggested that we cut through the paddy fields to get there faster. My dad grew up near those fields, so he was comfortable walking in the dark through the rice fields, and Pilan *chettan* could always masterfully navigate the paddy fields, even at night.

I was preoccupied with the snakes lurking in the still, shallow waters of the paddy fields. Even as these thoughts filled my mind, I wanted to go with my dad, and since he and Pilan *chettan* were with me, I convinced myself that I would be safe.

The moon was high in the sky that night and illuminated the landscape so that we could navigate the narrow, raised-dirt walkways between the paddy fields, which were divided into squares. During the twenty-minute walk (which seemed like an hour), I stayed close to my dad, scanning side to side in the moonlight at the water below the green rice chutes. I thought I saw a number of snakes slithering on the surface of the shallow water close to me, but both my dad and Pilan *chettan* told me that I was letting my imagination get the best of me. I wasn't so sure.

As we approached the entrance of the original Maliekal house where my dad grew up, he told me about the times he spent here as a boy and a young man. As we strolled through the front of the property with the moonlight coming through the coconut and palm trees above, it provided us with a good view of the spacious front yard. He pointed out to me all the trees and the pond that he used to play around when he was my age. He laughed as he joyfully retold the stories to Pilan *chettan* and me from his youth in this old house.

This main house and property had been in the Maliekal family for generations. I've tried numerous times to find out whether my dad's side or my mom's side of the family settled in Puthenchira first, but both families claim that honor. One thing is for sure: both my maternal and paternal families are old, established families in the area and have been living in Puthenchira for multiple generations.

As we approached the house, my hand rested in my dad's hand, and I couldn't help but feel elated. Even though I had only been with him for a few hours, I already felt that he really was my dad, and I was delighted that he was finally by my side.

When we arrived at the front door, my dad knocked and called out. "Lily, it's me, Xavier; open the door."

"Who is it?" answered my Aunt Theresa from just inside. Aunt Theresa was a savvy lady, and she was convinced that we were a band of thieves preying on two ladies staying alone at the house that evening. She was not about to open the door.

My mom tried to go by the window to look out, but my aunt pulled her back forcefully.

"Don't let them see you. They probably knew that you arrived tonight."

"Who is it?" I knew my mother's voice. She was thoroughly confused that someone was shouting claiming to be Xavier.

My aunt emphatically told her not to open the door, and that it was just someone waiting to steal the gold bangles and earrings that my mom was wearing.

It had been four long years since he had left for America, and through the howling wind that night, plus with the thick wooden door muffling his voice, my mom was not exactly sure who it was speaking outside claiming to be Xavier.

Knowing that it was Mom, I shouted to her to confirm. "Mommy, it's me and Daddy. Let us in".

My mom immediately recognized my voice and opened the door, even as my aunt tried to unsuccessfully intervene. They were met with the three of us in front of the house with the happiest smiles on our faces.

My mom's face lit up at the sight of my dad. "It's you! How come you didn't tell me that you were coming today?" she said with surprise.

After we stepped into the house, my dad explained to my mom about the telegram that he'd sent to my uncle, and how no one was waiting for him at the airport. But Mom still had a very confused look on her face. My dad continued to explain all that happened, but after a few minutes the explanations stopped because everyone was just thrilled to have my dad home.

As I looked up at my parents happily conversing and catching up, I felt an incredible sense of joy at seeing them together. I had only seen them together in pictures up until that moment. I only remember a few other moments from my dad's two-month-long visit that year, but that first night is etched into my mind.

About halfway into my dad's stay, we were told that we would be going to the nearest US Embassy in Madras.[5] Madras was in the state directly east of us, and it would require a ten-hour train journey to get the remaining paperwork sorted out so that my mom, brothers, and I could travel to America to join my dad in Chicago. Apparently, the authorization needed for us to go to America was ready, and my dad would be able to take us to join him. I didn't quite understand all of the details behind it or what it entailed, but I was excited about our overnight train journey, as it would be my first one. My friends told me that when going to Madras there would be a sleeper car, and we would get a room with bunk beds to ourselves.

When we finally got to the Chalakudy train station, it was as crowded as usual. The Indian railway system was one of the largest in the world, and it was the primary mode of transportation for long-distance travel within India.

As we got on the platform, which was brightly painted in a golden yellow with brown trim, I could see all sorts of people getting ready to board the express train to Madras. The station was buzzing with people moving around and vendors selling all sort of delicious fried treats on the platform. I asked my mom if I could get some, but she said that it would make me sick; and besides, they would feed us on the train.

After pushing our way through the door, we entered our very own

5   Madras, a name carried over from British rule, is a South Indian city now known as Chennai

compartment. It had two small bunk beds up above with seats on the bottom on either side. The seats on the bottom could also be converted into beds so that two individuals could sleep on the bottom. My brother James and I immediately jumped on the top beds and claimed them for ourselves.

The two small fans near the windows spun so fast it looked like the blades were going to fly out of the metal cage. The fans did keep the room somewhat cool, which was a welcome relief in the warm evening.

Soon after we settled into our compartment, the train left the platform. I peered out of the window and watched the station fly by us. After eating our meals, we were told to go to sleep. James and I climbed back up to the upper bunks and fell fast asleep, dreaming about going to America.

We arrived in Madras the next morning. I've never seen a place so full of cars, trucks, and people. We made our way to the hotel, and my dad told us to rest up, as we had a busy day tomorrow at the embassy.

With all of our needed documentation in hand, we took a taxi to the US embassy. I'd never set eyes on a place so big before in my life. The whole complex stretched out as far as my eyes could see, and all the buildings were white with many windows. They looked different from the ones in the surrounding area behind me. My dad mentioned to me that this was a little bit how America looked, so I paid more attention to the details and focused to absorb everything I saw.

There were fences everywhere, with perfectly manicured gardens and very modern-looking parked cars that I had never seen before. Until then, I had only seen Ambassador cars in my home town, which looked like giant turtles and were either black or white. Here, I saw colorful cars that were built low to the ground that looked like they were built for speed.

"They are Italian, and are called Fiats," explained my dad, as if on cue. We walked into the lobby to see a room spread out with numerous, colorful chairs: a stark contrast to the wooden, stiff-back chairs that I had seen before in Kerala homes.

After a while, my mother went into a separate interview room, and when she came back she had a big smile on her face, saying she passed. My dad had spoken with her the previous evening and was concerned that she would not answer all the questions properly with her broken English. My mom was always confident about everything, and she had told us that she would not have any problems with the questions. Even with her broken English, she was able to answer all the questions satisfactorily for the US immigration agent.

I thought that was it, and that we would be on our way back home to Puthenchira; I missed my grandmother and our home. But my dad told me that we all needed a medical check-up first. That was the first time I had heard of this; I hated to go to clinics or hospitals, and I *especially* hated getting shots. We got in another Ambassador taxi and were on our way to the clinic when I started questioning my mom about exactly what was going to happen next. You can understand my interest in the matter.

She declined to say and rightly so; had I known, I would have jumped out of the taxi and onto the street. I had to have three or four shots, and the doctor checked me every which way, including taking something he called "X-rays." I really felt like crying when I got the shots, but I tried to keep up a brave face because I did not want to look bad in front of my father. My brothers where howling so much that people across the main hall could hear them. My mom tried her best to reassure them, but they continued screaming even after the process was complete.

Finally, after what seemed to me to be an excessively long time, all the medical checks were completed and we went back to the embassy to get our final approval to be on our way to America. It was a long day, and Dad told us that we would be going to a restaurant for dinner that night. I quickly forgot about all of the day's activities, because this was my first dinner at a restaurant in a big city.

CHAPTER 5

THE VOYAGE

The backwaters of Kerala near Cochin, Kerala

Soon after we got back from Madras, my dad was preparing to leave again. I thought we would all be accompanying him when he went back to America, but apparently our passports and other clearances were going to take a few months longer. We said our goodbyes, knowing that we would be seeing him again soon.

I was then in fifth grade and, as we got closer to leaving, I had mixed feelings about leaving all my friends behind. In Kerala, English was taught as a second language, starting in fifth grade. So even though I could not complete it, it was timely for me to pick up at least a few words and phrases.

The morning of our travel to America came quickly. I was so excited about going that leaving my friends and relatives behind forever did not sink in for me that day. My grandmother's house was buzzing with activity with all our relatives and neighbors there. My uncle, Father Callistus, reviewed all the documents with my mom, and once again did a practice run on how she should answer questions in English at US customs once she reached New York. Always confident, my mom told him not to worry: she would be fine. I'm sure she was sad to leave her mother, her sister, and brother but she didn't show it.

I liked my Uncle Father Callistus when I was young, but he always seemed so busy and not as friendly as his older brother, my Uncle Father John. This was an unfair assessment of him when I was young, because despite not showing it, he was actually a giving man that not only helped his family but also the larger communities that he served as a priest. Only later in my life did I come to understand what an important figure Father Callistus was in my life, and to many other Maliekals that eventually emigrated to America.

I learned from my parents that Father Callistus was the first in the family to go to America back in 1958 in pursuit of his PhD in English Literature. He was admitted to Loyola University in Chicago and attended there until his graduation in 1962.

Father Callistus was a missionary priest who excelled at making contacts and persuading people to donate to worthy causes in India. Joseph was his baptized name, and he was the sixth of nine in my dad's family. I found out that he was a real troublemaker when he was young, but always adventurous. To the delight of my grandmother, he joined the priesthood and completed his studies in philosophy and theology. He was a professor of theology for a short period before making his way to Chicago.

My parents also mentioned that, following his studies in America, Father Callistus came back to India and helped build a modern church and college in Kerala, called Christ College, where he was an English professor in addition to all his missionary work. He was the first person from our rural village, which was situated in the furthest corner of India, to set foot in America.

One evening, my wife and I counted the number of individuals, siblings, children, and grandchildren that Father Callistus was directly responsible for coming to the US, and it was close to two hundred people. My wife had taken an interest in how the Maliekals arrived in Chicago and had already assembled many details on those connected to Father Callistus who had come to the US. I was surprised at all the information she had compiled about my family. She knew my side of the extended family better than I did.

Father Callistus made many friends and acquaintances while he was in Chicago. He once told me that he never forgot the face or the name of a person that he met. He had a sophisticated Rolodex where he kept all his contact information.

Rev. Fr. Callistus Maliekal, my dad's older brother, who came to Chicago in 1958 to pursue his PhD in English Literature at DePaul University—at a private audience with Pope Paul VI

After a few years in America, he knew Chicago well enough and had made enough connections to consider sponsoring my dad to come and study in America. My dad told me that it had always been his goal to make it out of our village and go to America one day. He had convinced his older brothers earlier to send him to Bombay (now known as Mumbai) for additional studies, and then eventually made it to Malaysia, where he was an assistant professor at a college. But his end goal was always to get to America.

After being pestered by my dad daily, Father Callistus initiated the process for my dad to go and study in Chicago on a student visa. He also managed to sponsor one of his nieces, Annie Maliekal, to also obtain a student visa to study in Chicago. They were the inaugural Maliekal family members that eventually established permanent residences in America and set the stage for many others to follow.

The first time I remember going to an airport was when we left for America. We arrived at Cochin airport early to make sure we didn't miss our flight. It was exhilarating seeing the planes and travelers at the airport. Cochin airport in 1969 was an old, converted military facility from WWII. It only had one main building and a single runway, but it looked gigantic to me. My mom mentioned that she and I had been there once before when we traveled to Malaysia to live with my dad. We had lived in Kuching, Malaysia for a few years, but I was too young to remember. My brother, James, was born there.

I kept pointing at the airplane that I saw taxiing down the runway, delighting in sharing the new sight with my brothers, and we were all in a jovial mood. Uncle Sunny and my mom scurried around to get all our luggage checked in and paperwork in order while the three of us followed closely behind with our mouths open and eyes staring in wonder. Uncle Sunny convinced the airport employees that he had to help his sister and family get settled on the plane, and he was allowed to accompany us, carrying our smaller bags all the way up to the entrance of the plane.

We waved our final goodbyes to my uncle and were on our way to be reunited with my dad in Chicago.

As we sat on the runway waiting to leave, my brothers and I suddenly wondered aloud at how exactly this heavy vessel would actually take off and fly. We all turned to Mom as the engines roared and the plane accelerated down the runway. I could sense the plane rumbling. My throat started to get dry, and my stomach started to ache. I looked out the window to focus on the scenery to take my mind off the plane's shaking. This helped a little. All I could see were the coconut trees, densely packed at the end of the runway near the water's edge.

The coconut trees had their familiar lean into the water, seeking sunlight. I researched this as an adult and discovered that even though most trees have trunks that will bend away from the wind, the coconut tree on the water's edge does the opposite. A trunk that leans downwind becomes less exposed and structurally built for surviving strong winds. But the coconut tree is sturdy, and bends towards the open sunlight. It does this because coconut trees like to grow as close to the water as possible. Even though many seeds from other plants are carried by wind or animals, coconuts are taken to start a new life elsewhere, often on another island, by sea currents.

As I pondered over this newfound information, I couldn't help but see the parallels of my own journey as a young boy, leaving behind the relatives that had nurtured me as a young boy in Kerala to head to a new land.

Once up in the air, the beauty of the backwaters came into full focus: they looked like a network of intricate loops shaded in jade. Little did I know that this iconic image of Kerala would be my last until I returned fifteen years later. The plane swayed and made all kinds of noise, but Mom assured us that it was all normal and that soon it would quiet down. However, I noticed that when she looked away from us she was nervously playing with her nails, and her face seemed strained although she spoke to us in reassuring tones. I only realized later that she had to put on a brave face for us. We had complete trust in her.

The trip from Cochin to Bombay was a short one, and we all enjoyed it because the air hostesses, who were dressed in beautiful, colorful saris, served us a refreshing lemonade drink and spicy peanuts during the flight. The landing brought with it another stressful few minutes for me as I looked anxiously out the window. I was thankful when we finally touched down on the ground. After coming to a stop, I could also see the relief in my brothers' eyes.

After we disembarked and reached the terminal, my brothers thought that we were already in America. Little did they know that it would be another thirty hours before we reach our American destination.

The plane we took from Bombay was even bigger, and the flight to London seemed to take forever. During the middle of the flight, my brother James was really impatient about not being able to get up and walk around as he pleased. He loudly whined at our mom. "I want to go back to Grandma's house right now," he insisted.

We did not like the western and North Indian food that was being served to us, as it was drastically different from what we were used to in Kerala. The one dish I still remember being served, small sausages and beans (which I later learned was pork & beans), brought up images of dog and goat poop back at my grandma's house. Not wanting to throw up, my brothers and I stuck to filling our stomachs with potato chips and Coke the entire trip.

After what seemed like a couple of days, we finally landed in London. The three of us were excited about stepping out in Heathrow airport. Unfortunately, my mom told us that we were going to just sit in the plane, because she did not want to get lost at the massive Heathrow airport. She was not about to take any chances when she was so close to reuniting all of us with my dad. Even though she had flown on a plane a few years back to Malayasia, she did not want to walk around with three young kids in tow and end up missing the connection.

Luckily, the TWA flight hostesses took pity on her after seeing the three of us at her side and allowed us to stay on the plane while it was being serviced for the next leg of the trip.

Soon we were in the air again, and the flight to New York seemed to take even longer than the last. The seats were uncomfortable, and my stomach hurt, so I did not sleep much. My brothers did not fare any better, with my mom marching them down to the bathroom frequently.

After being cooped up in the plane for what seemed like an eternity, my brothers and I had just about *had it*. I would keep asking my mom, "How much longer to get to Chicago?" She would always assure me that we would be there soon. I tried to pin her down to find out exactly how many hours more, but she kept dodging the question or responding with a vague answer.

My younger brothers took a different tactic: they didn't ask how much longer, but only how they could leave right then and get back to our grandma's house.

I was finally able to sleep a little towards the end of the flight, and when I woke up we had arrived in New York. I could tell by the look on her face that my mom did not get a wink of sleep with my little brothers crying and wanting to go to the bathroom the whole trip. She looked tired, but she was watching over us closely as we made our way down the bridge. I have a lot of admiration for my mom, who single-handedly trekked my two little brothers and I on a thirty-six-hour voyage over multiple planes all the way to America.

We had finally arrived in New York at JFK airport, and all I can remember are all the red chairs in the gate area as we finally made our way out of the plane. It took forever to get through customs, and we were completely exhausted from the trip. But as soon as we saw my dad outside Immigration, our spirits soared, and we felt energized. He had taken an earlier flight to New York so that we would able to fly together to Chicago. My mother was relieved that Dad joined us in New York, and even though we got rerouted on our way to Chicago because of some mechanical problems, the trip seemed a lot easier now that Dad was with us.

It seemed like ages since we had left my grandma's house, but finally we arrived in Chicago. Two tall white men who were friends of my dad met us at the gate area, and we all boarded a car with one of the new men driving. We were on our way to our new house.

Unfortunately, it was early evening in the middle of winter, so I could not really see anything out the window except for the dazzling array of dancing white lights beaming at us on one side of the road and the red lights in front of us. I realized I would have to wait until we get to the house to see what America was all about. I got bored and sleepy watching all the twinkling white and red lights of the cars and trucks on the road, so I settled in on my mom's shoulder and took a small nap.

PART II: NEW SOIL

CHAPTER 6

"SWEET HOME CHICAGO"

My first summer in Chicago next to our family car across from
our house on Wood street—July 1970

M y family stepped into our new home that cold, snowy December
evening, and Dad proudly set the mood with his hands spread out
wide, optimism in his voice. "Here's our new home. What do you think?"

It was a modest two-bedroom apartment, but compared to what I
had been used to, it looked foreign and very organized. The space was
nothing like any homes in Kerala. The walls and floors were sterile-looking
compared to my grandmother's house. Despite this, I was curious to be
somewhere new, and thought it was time to check the place out. My
dad immediately started showing us all the conveniences that this home
had versus where we had lived back in Kerala. From electric lights and

running water to automated appliances, he pointed out many items that were unfamiliar to us. I wondered if anyone actually needed to work in American homes, since everything was done by machines.

My dad then took my brothers and I to show us our new bedroom. It was a small room near the dining room table. My mom thought it would be good for me to sleep with my little brother Joe, who was only five years old, so that he wouldn't be scared at night. There were two beds, and we all agreed that my little brother and I would sleep on the right side and my brother James on the left.

The three of us sat on the beds, and we couldn't believe how soft they were. It was not a big room, but we had it all to ourselves, and over the next five years it was in this little bedroom that we spent a lot of time talking, laughing, and even fighting, on occasion.

After first seeing the bedroom, we stepped back out into the dining area to continue the tour. There was a big contraption with a small window and blue flames inside. There was also a big pipe sticking out that extended into the ceiling. When I asked my dad what this was, he told me that it was our heater, which provided warmth during the winter.

Our apartment was kept habitable during the frigid winter months by this one heating unit sitting in our dining room. Luckily our bedroom was not too far away, and it would keep the three of us warm while we slept. But the farther you were away from it, the more the temperature dropped.

We followed Dad as the tour continued, and he went up the single step leading to the living room. It contained a small, rectangular box, which I knew was a TV from the pictures I had seen back in India. My dad turned it on, and my brothers and I were mesmerized by the black and white images and voices coming out of the box. We all sat down on the floor right in front of the screen.

The first show I remember seeing was the comedy show *The Munsters*.

It was an incredibly strange show, where the actors were all dressed in weird costumes. We couldn't make out exactly who they were supposed to be, but we loved it. My brothers and I had a hard time following the show, but we still enjoyed our very first television experience. We were not exposed to scary creatures like Frankenstein and vampires back in India; the only scary creatures in Puthenchira were animals, like snakes and rabid dogs.

My mom was excited to see that the kitchen was equipped with a gas stovetop and a large fridge, not to mention running water. My dad showed her how the range worked. I was pleasantly surprised to see the fridge full of food. These were common items across all houses in America, but this was extravagance for someone from the village of Puthenchira, India, in 1969.

After getting a tour of our first American apartment, we all sat down, and my dad treated us to snacks, including our first bottle of RC Cola and Jays potato chips, which I found out later were both Chicago originals.

We were tired from the long trip, so we went to sleep early that first night. I slept soundly, and the next thing I knew it was morning. My brothers and I were filled with anticipation to see our new home and our new neighborhood during the daytime. By morning, the snow that had started the previous evening was already about a foot high. Everywhere we looked out the window was covered in white. The trees and their branches looked as if someone had covered them all with fluffy cotton. The sun was shining though the partial blue sky, and the voluptuous snow on the branches perfectly matched the sporadic cloud patterns in the sky. As we sat and stared out the window, looking at the beautiful snowscape, a heavenly aroma filled our noses.

My dad was busy making breakfast for us, with Mom watching closely to observe the workings of the new kitchen. They called us in, and we found my dad cooking something in the frying pan. We thought he was frying dried fish, like we would do back in Puthenchira, but he said it was bacon.

We then had our fill of egg omelets and the newly-discovered bacon (which we all liked) and we were about to go outside to play in the snow when our landlady's son, who lived below her in the main building, came to see us. Mr. Stanley was accompanied by his two daughters, Claudia and Gracie. They introduced themselves and talked mostly with my dad while my mom, brothers, and I remained silent. They seemed friendly. I tried listening attentively, but I did not understand much of what they were saying. It was like they were speaking with marbles in their mouths, as it all seemed muffled to me.

I couldn't help but notice how tall the two girls were, as they were both slightly taller than my dad and towered over me. They also both had golden hair, which I had seen on a few girls at the airport but never so close up. I thought the younger girl, Claudia, who was probably five or six years older than me and about a foot taller, was beautiful with her long, wavy golden hair.

Later that day we also went to see our landlady, Mr. Stanley's mom, who was extremely kind. She was a heavyset lady with snow-white hair. When she spoke, she became animated and energetic. She talked to us through Dad, who translated everything for us. She told my brothers and me that we should call her "Grandma," since my dad had told her that we had lived in our grandma's house back in India and that we missed her very much. She gave the three of us sweets and told us that we were welcome at her place any time.

Our new grandma was one of the nicest ladies I had ever met during the time that we lived there, and I thought to myself that if everyone in America were as nice as her, we would be in good shape. She always had a good word to say to us, and on our birthdays she would give the three of us a gift of fifteen dollars, which at the time was a quarter of our monthly rent.

After a few days we went to one of my dad's Indian friends' house, who was from our home state. He and his wife came to our place to pick us up, and then we drove to theirs. Our new uncle and aunty showed us their house and took us shopping to buy winter coats, gloves, and scarves at a nearby shopping center.

I couldn't believe how many stores there were under one roof. Shopping malls were not in Kerala yet, so the shopping complex was another new discovery. It was a strange feeling to try on all the winter gear. I couldn't move with all the heavy clothing on me, and I felt shackled and constricted. My dad picked out winter clothing for all of us, and we were on our way. We didn't really care too much about the clothing stores, but my brothers and I had our mouths open as we went by the toy stores in the mall.

Later that week, one of my dad's nieces and her family came to see us. It was Annie Maliekal, who had come to the US a few days prior to my dad after my uncle, Father Callistus, had also sponsored her student visa in 1964 so she could study in Chicago. Aunt Annie was also from Puthenchira. After completing her studies, she married an American and settled with her family on the west side of Chicago.

She is an incredibly smart and courageous woman, who set out for a new life in Chicago as a single woman. She eventually married a gentleman named Bob, a native Chicagoan, and they had two children at the time of her visit. I always had a lot of respect for Aunt Annie because an Indian woman traveling alone to study in the US was unheard of. But she was bright and capable, as my uncle had correctly predicted prior to sponsoring her. She was able to settle down with her family in Chicago while also helping her family back in India.

She went on to have four more children, and I even had the honor being a godfather to their youngest child, Nancy. I was only eighteen at the time, and didn't think much of it then, but now that I'm older I'm proud that there's a special connection between Nancy and I. A number of Aunt Annie's brothers and sisters eventually settled in the US through her sponsorships.

Uncle Bob, as we called her husband, was one of the friendliest people I remember growing up us a child in Chicago. My fondest memory of him was the Bobby Hull hockey game that he gave my brothers and me one Christmas. The game was similar to foosball, but with a hockey puck and skaters strategically positioned on the miniature rink just like in a real game. I never thought I would have a game like this, and we played it for years before it finally broke down.

I can't help but think frequently about the Maliekal pioneers who came to the US like Aunt Annie and my dad when there were few Indians in America, let alone from our home state of Kerala. I can only imagine the initial struggles they overcame adapting to a colder climate, conversing in English, and trying to adjust to a way of life that was totally foreign to them. My brothers and I also had to adapt to the new language and culture, but it was much simpler for us because we were young and received constant care and encouragement from our parents.

Christmas came that year, and it was wonderful. Dad went out to buy a real Christmas tree, and we learned that we could decorate it. We celebrated Christmas in India, but back in Kerala, instead of a Christmas tree every Christian family made a small manger to commemorate the birth of Jesus. There were no gifts exchanged back in India, and we were thrilled that when people came to see us in Chicago, they came bearing gifts.

We also ate a lot of food that first month, including chicken and beef, which were plentiful in comparison to Puthenchira. Back in India, we only had meat maybe once or twice a week, but here we had it every day.

My dad was happy to see the three of us who were very thin eat heartily. My mom still prepared all the food Indian style, as we weren't quite ready for the American versions just yet. We also enjoyed Coke, potato chips, and fresh fruits. I remember my brother claiming how back in India Grandma would only give us one slice of apple each, whereas now Dad gave us a whole apple to ourselves every night.

We also watched TV quite a bit, since this was completely new to the three of us. *Gilligan's Island*, *The Brady Bunch*, *Speed Racer*, and many other programs were always on during those early years in Chicago. The TV became our portal into learning American culture, and was also a great tool to learn English.

My dad then told us about school and how we were enrolled to start as soon as the New Year came. My parents were concerned about enrolling us into American schools in the middle of a schoolyear.

"I am considering stepping both you and James back one year so that you could get better at English," said Dad.

I objected to this right away. "You can't make me go back to 4th grade. I already passed 4th grade with straight A's!"

"That was in Puthenchira," said Mom, "and this is an English school in America; your English still needs a lot of work."

I looked around to James to see if he was going to say anything to back me up, but he really was not listening, instead watching TV with my little brother. He was only a second grader at the time, so I'm not sure he grasped the full impact of this decision.

"You can't do that!" I continued, pleading against this truly unjust direction my schooling was about to take. "Everyone will make fun of me; and besides, I did real well in my last English class." Even though the class I was referring to was the introductory English taught at our school to all 5th graders, I really thought I could get by.

"Please don't step me back," I pleaded, beginning to cry. "I will do well, don't worry."

James finally came to back me up, and entered the conversation shouting. "If George is going to be in 5th grade then I want to be in 2nd grade just like I was back in India!" He immediately went back to watching *Speed Racer*.

My little brother, Joseph, was only five years old at the time, so this decision really had no impact on him, since he would only start first grade the following year. He and James were glued to *Speed Racer*, which was a popular cartoon that we watched daily.

I could see the TV screen out of the corner of my eye as Speed raced against the dreaded Car Acrobatic Team. I badly wanted to join them to see how Speed would fare against his arch-rival Snake Oiler, but I had to get resolution on the school issue.

After some more tears and pleading from me, my parents finally agreed on 5th grade with the caveat that they would judge my progress at the end of the year and determine if I should repeat 5th grade again the following year.

As I walked away to join my brothers, I couldn't believe that my parents did not think I could do it. I didn't say anything more, figuring that I had already gotten what I wanted, and anything more I said could have them rethinking their decision. I decided right then and there that there was no way I was going to repeat 5th grade again. That night, I started thinking about what school in America would be like and started getting anxious about meeting my new American classmates.

Although I was anxious about starting at a new school when I knew so little English, I was motivated to pass 5th grade and determined to show my parents that I was capable.

It was only a few years later that I realized I would be in some cases twelve to fifteen months younger than my classmates because of my later birthday and the American school calendar differences from the school calendar in India. This put me at a size disadvantage throughout my elementary and high school years, but ultimately I became wiser because of it.

CHAPTER 7

CONTACT

St. Boniface church and elementary school.
Attended from 1970-73

I was driving down the Kennedy Expressway a few years ago, headed to
downtown Chicago to see a concert with my good friend Gary Klawans,
whom I've known for forty years.

Off in the distance I could see a familiar sight approaching, and the
always-stunning Chicago skyline came into view. I never get tired of
seeing that view. The John Hancock building and the Sears Tower are
the two I identify with the most. These two buildings majestically rise up
from the ground, towering over the city. They are befitting of Chicago's
nickname "The City of Big Shoulders." I was fortunate enough as a young
boy growing up in Chicago in the early seventies to be able to enjoy these

two magnificent 20th century skyscrapers when they were two of the tallest in the world for many years.

Even though it was not as tall as the Sears tower, the John Hancock building (originally named after a prominent patriot of the American Revolution) has always been my favorite, since it was close to my high school on the edge of Lake Michigan. I admire the wide stance of the base and the angle of it as it rises to the clouds. The all-black profile, with diamond-shaped bracing that runs on the face of the building, gives it a bold look. I frequently stare at this geometrical structure as it aches to touch the sky. I can be hypnotized for minutes on end.

The John Hancock building also has the best view of the city because it is near the lake. It is always an amazing sight from the observation deck on a sunny day, with Oak Street beach fronting Lake Michigan on one side, and the city laid out in all its glory on the other three sides. Prior to 2000, I frequently told visitors who wanted to go to the Sears Tower because it was the tallest building in the world that they would be better off going to the John Hancock building, because it would be a much better sightseeing experience due to its proximity to Lake Michigan. These days, both the names of the buildings have changed due to new owners, but I can't help referring to these buildings by their original names.

I reduced my speed slightly on the Kennedy Expressway due to traffic as we approached Augusta Boulevard on the near west side of Chicago. The narrow, reddish-brown tower with its black triangular roof came into view, and I started reminiscing to Gary about it.

"Hey, there's St. Boniface. That's where I went to grade school when I first came to the US." I found myself continuing on in that line of thought, telling him that the original school was torn down years ago and now only the church was still standing, despite being vacant for a decade. The last time I went to see the church, there were pigeons flying inside and the interior looked like it had been through a tornado. It was an incredibly sad sight to see, since back in its prime the interior of the church had held dozens of colorful statues of saints and a decorative ceiling with exquisitely painted religious figures.

"I didn't realize you lived this close to downtown when you came to the US," commented Gary.

"This was a great area growing up, but the neighborhoods have gone through many changes," I answered back.

Gary is also a native Chicagoan and grew up a little farther north, so he knew the neighborhoods well. He went on to mention that my parents should've held onto the house here because it would be worth a mint now, what with the property values of land near downtown skyrocketing.

My old neighborhood was full of rebuilt condos and townhomes with a few of the old houses sprinkled in between. Many young professionals take advantage of the proximity to the downtown area while enjoying a diverse city neighborhood. I reminded him that we were renting at that time; we were just starting out in America back when we arrived in December of 1969.

Passing the building as we made our way downtown on the Kennedy, I took a quick look back at St. Boniface in my rearview mirror and couldn't help but think back to my first day there.

It was January, 1970. I stood in front of the 5th grade class at St. Boniface with Sister Clarine and many strange faces looking back at me. As I peered out to my future classmates, I wondered if my dad was right about stepping me back a grade. They all looked so much bigger and older than me.

Sister Clarine turned to me with a friendly smile. "Class, this is our new student, George; he just came from India. He will be joining us in 5th grade. He's a good student and had really good grades in all his subjects, so I'm sure he will do well here. George, would you like to say hello to the class?"

I stood there, dumbfounded, because I could not understand anything she was saying. I made out a few words, but the rest sounded like she was far away and mumbling: very similar to the adults in the *Peanuts* cartoons on TV that my brothers and I saw during Christmas.

Sister Clarine was a tall, older nun with glasses, dressed in a drab brown garment with a traditional black veil on her head. She seemed thin for her height, and whenever she spoke to me I could smell some remnant of horrible, cooked vegetable on her breath. In the days previous, my dad and mom helped me with common phrases in English and tried to prepare me for my first day of class, but I was too frightened to respond to the tall, skinny nun with the celery breath.

Everyone waited for me to say something in the deafening silence of the classroom. I just stood there, staring at Sister Clarine, not knowing what to do. Then I heard someone in the class mumble something with a grin on his face. Others in the class started to laugh.

Sister Clarine immediately asked the boy who had mumbled to come up and extend his right hand. I knew this drill because back in India the nuns were always hitting students in the palm of the hand with a wooden yardstick if they did something wrong. Fortunately for me, all it took was one time in second grade, and I never did anything again to warrant a ruler strike from the teacher on the open face of my hand.

As he came up and stood near me, I looked like a midget next to Sister Clarine and this huge 5th grader. He looked like he should be in the Indian secondary school, or high school here in America.

She stepped behind her desk and took out a long, wooden ruler. She gave a slight whack to his extended right hand. I noticed this kid immediately extended and flexed his hand and then went back to his desk. This was not the first time. I didn't think she hit him as hard as the nuns back in India, but he winced a bit.

"And now we will have none of that." She faced the rest of the class and sternly told them, "And that goes for the rest of you, also." At that point I knew that he must have said something bad, but I didn't really think it was directed at me, so I just kept standing in the front of the class looking like I was ready to throw up.

Sister Clarine finally took pity on me and turned to me, pointing to my desk. "You can go back to your desk now, George." She said this much slower, and I was able to make out most of it. I definitely heard the words "go" and "desk" and I was thrilled that I didn't have to stay in front of the class anymore. I quickly walked back to my desk and sat down. I was glad to have that episode behind me.

As I sat back down, dejected, with tears welling up in my eyes, I thought to myself that this could be a lot harder than I thought.

The rest of the morning was not much better, as I did not understand much of what was said when we covered Social Studies and English. Luckily, I was able to read a little bit of what was written in the Social Studies and English books, but I still could not understand sister Clarine fully when she spoke. Every time she glanced at me she would instinctively speak slower, but soon after would be back to her rapid talking.

When it came time for lunch, Sister Clarine helped me to pick out a few things to eat and sat with me and the other kids while we ate. I didn't like too much of what was on my plate, but I drank down my first carton of chocolate milk, which was delicious. I looked around to see how I could get another, as I was still hungry. I didn't see anyone else going for a second one, so I finished up and threw most of my lunch in the garbage. I scurried behind Sister Clarine back to our classroom.

In the afternoon, the only bright spot was when we covered math. Even though I could not understand much of what was being said, I was able to follow along with the math problems on the blackboard, and when it came time for us to solve the problems, I thought I always finished first. I also felt great whenever sister Clarine came and looked over my shoulder to smile and praise me.

"Very good, George." I understood this phrase, and I felt great whenever she said it.

After school, I walked towards my mom, who had come to pick me and my brother up. My classmates did not say much. I got the feeling this was their first time seeing an Indian kid in class, and they weren't sure how to react.

But one boy from my class ended up shouting and waving. "See you tomorrow in class, George!" he said cheerfully. He turned and walked away. Before I could wave back, he was already lost among the crowd of kids milling around the entrance of the school, so I left with my mom and brothers.

As we were stepping out into the sidewalk, I saw a bunch of older kids across the street gliding on ice in an open space with sticks in their hand. They all had colorful uniforms, but I couldn't figure out what they were doing. I asked my mom what it was, but she said she had no idea and quickly turned away and told us to start walking. I made a mental note to ask Dad as soon as we got home. To this day I still remember all the details of that visual, as it was the inception of my passion for the game of hockey.

My parents did not have a car yet, and the walk back home was cold. It was a crisp, sunny day, and my brothers and I tried to match my mom's quick purposeful stride. My little brother Joseph, who had come along with her, had some trouble keeping up, so I would give him a little push to help him along.

As we made the right turn from Chestnut to Ashland Avenue, I could smell the wonderful aroma of the bakery on the corner. We all had our heads down as we fought the chilling winds of January in Chicago, but I managed to take a quick peek at the vertical, dark green sign with white lettering. "Augusta Bakery," it read.

"Can we go in there and get something to eat? I'm hungry," I asked Mom, tugging on her coat.

"Didn't you get lunch at school?"

"I got it, but I didn't like any of it. It tasted terrible."

Both my brothers also smelled the goodies at Augusta Bakery as we stared wild-eyed at all the pastries displayed in the picture window. We were slowly passing the window, inspecting all the treats, and my brothers also chimed in that they wanted something to eat. We could all see beautiful cakes displayed, and they had trays and trays full of pastries that looked like Indian *vadas*[6] with a hole in the center; but unlike *vadas*, these had different things on top, including chocolate and white icing. Our mouths were watering as we stared at the tempting sweets in the window, but my mother stepped in to direct us away from them.

"We will get home soon, and I will cook all of you a nice, hot dinner." That was the end of that. When my mom said something *that* firmly it meant she was not going to change her mind. We made our way down Ashland Avenue and continued on home in the cold.

The next morning, James and I again walked our approximately one-mile hike to school with our mom and little brother in tow. My mom was not yet ready to send the two of us out on our own to walk to school.

The first week of school finally ended, and we were happy to get a couple of days off. Each day in school got a little bit better, and a few of the kids started talking to me. The boy who had waved to me on that first day sat with me at lunch, and spoke to me frequently. I found out his name was Gary Sylvie. I even picked up the nerve to try a little of my English and, even though it was not the smoothest conversation, we were communicating.

Gary was one of the coolest guys I've ever met, and to this day we are still friends. He was friendly, smart, and it was clear to see from day

---

6   In India, a vada is a fried, donut-like treat made from a type of lentil.

one that everyone in class had a lot of respect for him. He had a real calm to his demeanor as he went about his day. Many kids made fun of each other by calling names or just goofing around, but not once did I see Gary engage in any of this. I quickly decided that he would be a good person to learn from about how to get along at this school, and I tried hard to absorb as much as I could from him. He and I got along so well that he started teaching me the ropes, and he would always call me "little buddy."

Gary Sylvie was my first American friend, whom I met at our elementary school. We also attended high school together and remain friends. Circa 1974

It turns out that he had a brother and four sisters also going to the same school, so there was a Sylvie in almost every grade. Gary and his family lived nearby, and my mom and his mom also became friends as they participated in various events at the school.

After a few weeks in school I was starting to do better in my classes, but I still did not understand everything in the various subjects other than math class. I was easily one of the best students in math, but I continued to struggle in the other classes due to my deficient English skills.

One day, as we were working on a class assignment in Social Studies,

I did not quite understand the directions on the top of the page, so I asked the boy sitting next to me if he could explain it to me. This kid never paid much attention to me, so I was a little surprised that he responded and was trying to be helpful. He told me, "Go up to Sister Clarine and ask, '*What is this bullshit?*' She will then explain it to you."

Since I was still confused about the assignment, I thought this was the way you ask to clear things up. I had never heard of the word 'bullshit,' but then again, my English vocabulary at the time was limited to maybe twenty-five words, so I practiced saying it on the way up to the front. I said exactly what the boy, Carlos, told me.

Sister Clarine immediately went pale as a ghost and gave me a stern look; that was when I knew that I had been double-crossed.

I just stared at her helplessly, not knowing what to say. She quickly realized that I did not really know what I was saying, so she took me aside and mentioned to me that what I said was not appropriate language to use in school.

I told her that I was sorry and pointed to the assignment page directions with a puzzled look. I turned my right hand to gesture, *what does it mean?* She took the time to explain the assignment in further detail, and I went back to my desk. Feeling embarrassed, I glared at Carlos on my way to sit down, but he just chuckled.

During recess later that day, I saw an animated Gary speaking with Carlos who then came over to me. He put his hand on my shoulder. "Hey George, I was just joking," he said by way of an apology. I realized that Gary had come to his little buddy's aid, and I was grateful.

After a couple of weeks of going to school and staying near our home on the weekend, my brother James and I ventured out into the neighborhood on our own. As we turned away from our apartment entrance, we saw a number of kids playing in the narrow road behind the houses. We found out this was called "the alley," and my dad told us prior to heading out not to venture too far out from the alley.

One kid from the group came near us and invited us to join them. "Hey, do you guys want to play hockey with us?"

We looked behind us, thinking he was talking to someone else, but he came closer and continued, making it clear he really did mean *us*. "My name is Jimmy; what are your names?"

My brother was not about to say anything, so I spoke for both of us and answered quietly. "George, and my brother James."

"Do you guys want to play hockey with us?" Jimmy asked.

I had seen some ice hockey on TV because my dad was a fan, and he explained to me that what I had seen that first day at school was older kids playing hockey at an outdoor ice rink at the park across from our school. I did not know you could also play hockey in an alley.

"No sticks," I said while extending both my hands and gesturing how hockey players on TV held a hockey stick. We then quickly made our way home. Jimmy gave a shoulder shrug and headed back to the group of kids he was playing with.

"Playing hockey sounds really fun," James mentioned to me on the way home.

"I think so, too. We'll ask Dad about getting us some hockey sticks," I said. I didn't know where hockey sticks came from, but I figured Dad would know.

The next day was a Sunday, so we headed over to the alley one more time.

Jimmy was there again and called out to us. "Hey, do you guys live there?" He pointed at our house on the side of the street. We nodded our heads in unison.

Jimmy revealed a pair of extra hockey sticks he was carrying and persisted in his bid to get us to play with a generous offer. "George, we have a couple of extra sticks for you and your brother. So why don't you play with us?"

How could we refuse? I looked at James and he nodded his head, and we joined in.

They were desperate for additional players because it was a little tough to play hockey with only two kids on each side. It was then that we also met Jimmy's younger brother, who was named Memo. I thought it was a strange English name, but then again I'd heard a lot of strange names at school. I also met their cousin Alex and a neighbor kid named Boomer. All of them were about a head taller than I was, except for Alex, who was only six years old.

Jimmy and I were the oldest, but you wouldn't know it by looking at us. With the exception of Alex, they were a lot taller and heavier than my brother and I. They were pleasant and happy that they had more players in the neighborhood to play hockey.

My brother and I split up and went to two different teams. James was a little nervous, but I told him he would be alright.

We tried the sticks. It was a little awkward, and we weren't good at handling or shooting the puck, but it was fun to play and make a few friends. They were patient with us and showed us how to hold our sticks. They didn't mind that we spoke in broken English. Jimmy later told me that his family was from Mexico, so they were used to hearing broken English from their family members.

After about thirty minutes, I told them that we had to go back. We felt really good running back as we saw Dad waving us in from the end of the alley on our street. We waved goodbye to our new friends, knowing that we would be back.

We went home that night pleading with my dad to buy us hockey sticks. We told him about buying sticks with a super blade, which our new friends had informed us were ideal for street hockey.

"Is it really a good idea for you to go out into the cold weather and play in the alley?" asked my mom.

"They are kids our age from school, and they play every afternoon in the cold weather," both James and I said in unison.

I added for extra measure, "We like the cold weather; it doesn't bother us anymore." I actually did *not* like the cold weather, but I definitely wanted to play hockey with our new neighbors again.

My dad stepped in and said that the next time we went shopping he would buy us sticks, as long as they weren't too expensive. He was a pretty big hockey fan already, and he was happy that we'd made a few friends in the neighborhood.

CHAPTER 8

REUNITED

Mom, Dad, my brothers James, Joseph, and I (left to right) in our yard

I was happy that my dad understood our desire to play street hockey with our new friends, because we were getting tired of the endless routine of coming home from school, watching TV, doing our homework, and going to sleep.

I was also extremely happy to have a dad around permanently, as he seemed to know everything about how things worked in America. He was also very good in English, and he taught us basic grammar rules each night. He wanted to make sure that his three sons learned the language quickly so that we could interact with Americans.

With all the TV that we watched, our English improved steadily in a just few months. It was slow, because I remember having to first comprehend what the other person said, translate to my native tongue, Malayalam, and then speak in English back. Initially it was exhausting, but we had learned to speak and comprehend enough to effectively communicate with our friends in the neighborhood and in school.

My brothers and I studying on our dining room table
with Mom watching from the kitchen

It was around this time when I learned that my dad's college major was English, both in India and America. He had come to the US as a student. He was sponsored by my uncle, Father Callistus, and enrolled at DePaul University in Chicago to pursue his master's degree in English Literature.

When he came to Chicago in 1964, there were not many Indians in Chicago, let alone people from the state of Kerala. He could not really work for income on a student visa, so he had to live frugally using his savings. He had a small apartment near the corner of Wabash Street and Chicago Ave in downtown Chicago, and he roomed with two of his friends from Kerala who were also in the country as students. Fortunately, my mom and dad had saved up some money from his teaching position that he'd had in Kuching, Malaysia, where he had taught for three years.

To help with some of the expenses, he somehow secured a part-time job at Marshall Field & Company at the downtown store one summer. I could never imagine my dad as a stock boy, but that was his job. He was not exactly the type to get his hands dirty, but I guess when you had to put food on the table you did what you had to. The downtown Marshall Field's was not too far away from where he lived. I still remember the first time I saw the store, when he took us there the summer after we had arrived in Chicago.

The Marshall Field & Company Building, which was built in two stages and completed construction in 1906, was the flagship location of the chain of department stores. Mr. Marshall Field was an influential businessman in Chicago from one of the wealthiest families.

My first view of the greenish-gray building left a lasting impression, and I could not believe a department store located in downtown Chicago could take up an entire city block. It took us thirty minutes to see all the picture windows beautifully displayed on all four sides of the store. As we walked around the store, it was hard to miss the distinctive outdoor clocks on each corner of the store and the elaborate, decorative architecture of the building.

After seeing some of the beautiful picture windows, some filled with interesting toys that we had never seen before, we asked our dad if we could go in. He replied that we could only stay for a little while, but we could go in.

The inside of Marshall Field's downtown store, which was one of the largest stores in the world, was even more impressive. The beautiful chandelier suspended from the ceiling in the main hall, which I later found out was designed by Tiffany & Co., and the vaulted, mosaic ceiling were both mesmerizing to see. The store had all types of beautiful clothing.

When we asked Dad where the toy department was, he just mentioned that this store was expensive, and then we were quickly on our way to the exit. He knew that if the three of us got to the toy department, we would never want to leave and would be begging him to buy something that he could not afford.

Interestingly enough, during my college days I also worked at Marshall Field and Company. I worked in one of the northern Chicago suburban stores, but one summer I worked in the same downtown store that my dad had worked. I was proud of this connection that my dad and I shared during our college years, though I'm sure his life was lot more hectic than mine was when working at Marshall Fields.

The downtown Marshall Field building was declared a National Historic Landmark and listed on the National Register of Historic Places on June 2, 1978, and it was designated a Chicago Landmark on November 1, 2005.

My entire family shopped at Marshall Field's frequently when I was older, especially with my discount when I worked there. We were all disappointed when Marshall Field's sold their stores to Macy's in 2008. I still stop in my tracks at the sight of the downtown store, and the building and surroundings have become one of my favorite places to photograph in Chicago. Every once in a while I will take out-of-town visitors inside the store, but I refuse to buy anything from Macy's.

My dad had his struggles adapting to a new culture without his family in Chicago. His master's classes were difficult, and the cold weather really bothered him, but he was persistent and he obtained his degree in 1968. After graduation, he taught high school English at Mendel Catholic high school in Chicago, but he did not enjoy it, so he decided to change careers after a few years. With his effective communication skills, he was able to move into a sales management role at a scientific supply company.

It was tough having an English major for a dad, because every paper we wrote for class was heavily scrutinized, and we always ended up doing multiple iterations. As difficult as it was facing Dad with my first draft, my grades in English did improve.

Later in life I came to find out that our middle names, which we had gone by in India, were namesakes for western authors. He named me Lean after British author Edward Lean. My brother's middle name was Green, after British author Roger Green, and my little brother's middle name was Jean after the American author Jean Toomer, since he was born while my dad was in Chicago. Lean, Green, and Jean were the names we were known as back in India. I'm not sure many people in India knew that our names came from famous authors from both England and America.

My parents decided that in America we would be known by our given first names on our birth certificates instead of our middle names. They thought this would help us assimilate better into American society.

My dad was a laid-back person who would always be telling us funny stories; but you did not want to get him mad, because then his belt came off, and we usually got a few whacks. On numerous occasions my brothers and I deserved it, because the three of us were hell on wheels when at home together. We were all quiet and respectful outside the house, but something about the three of us cooped up in that small apartment on the near west side of Chicago brought out the worst in us.

My dad was a master storyteller, and one of the funniest stories that I remember to this day is about his first American dinner outside in a restaurant. It was with my Uncle Father Callistus after he had recently arrived in the US in 1964.

My dad's stories always took time to tell because he usually gave a lot of background detail and managed to tell you about six or seven other things before getting to the point. Whenever he talked, he always got animated when telling us his stories. If you had the patience to listen to the whole story (which I always didn't), they were funny.

Out of the many stories he told us, the one below is the only one I remember completely, and I wanted to share it. The story epitomized my dad's sense of humor germane to everyday life, and it is something that I frequently mention to friends and family.

He began the tale with a hearty laugh, throwing his head back with tears of laughter in his eyes because he was already thinking about the punch line. We were all just sitting around one night after dinner on a cold, wintry Friday night when he started off by saying to me, "Did I ever tell you about my first night out at a restaurant in Chicago with your Uncle Father Callistus?"

I mumbled a faint "No," thinking to myself, *Oh boy, not another story.* My brothers quickly ran off into the other room to watch TV, and I was about to join them when my mom shot me a look to stay and listen.

My dad was in a good mood that night because it was the start of the weekend, so I figured I could listen for a few minutes, knowing that it was probably going to take twenty minutes or more. I decided to stick it out anyway without complaining.

He prefaced the story by telling me about the different types of food that he saw at the restaurant. Father Callistus knew how to order, so he picked out a chicken dish with vegetables for my dad. However, Dad had not liked the chicken or vegetables because both dishes were bland and nothing like the spicy food he was used to back in Kerala. He ended up reluctantly swallowing some of the food just to make his older brother happy.

"So after that terrible dinner," my father continued, "the waitress came over and asked me if I wanted tea or coffee."

He then stopped and looked at me with a puzzled look. He must have read the bored expression on my face, and he quickly tried to regather my interest. "No, just listen. This is funny," he assured me.

I'm glad I stuck it out, because what followed was his telling of his very first cup of tea he'd had in America.

"When our waitress came around to see if either one of us wanted coffee or tea," he said, "I was thinking, *Okay, great: something that will really hit the spot on a cold night.*

"'I'll have some tea, Miss,' I said, not knowing what was to come. My brother chimed in to have the waitress bring some cream and sugar, since he knew that's the way I liked tea.

"After a few minutes, the waitress brought a tea cup filled with hot water, a saucer, some packets on a plate, and a small container of milk. I was a little puzzled, because this was not the way I was used to getting tea in India or in Malaysia. Usually the tea came in a small pot with tea leaves inside for brewing, and then you would transfer it to the cup and add milk and sugar. So I turned to Father Callistus and asked for his direction in this new, foreign method of tea-making.

"'Where's the tea pot to brew the tea?' I said. Now, my brother was always busy doing something, and in that moment he was a little distracted while he looked through some paperwork in his briefcase.

"'Oh, you just make the tea in the cup with the tea bag that they have provided,' he explained. He pointed to the little packet with a small string attached to it. I was not sure exactly how it worked, but I figured we were in America so I assumed they must've come up with something I didn't know about. So I tore open the tea bag and placed all the tea leaves that were in the bag into the cup of hot water.

"Father Callistus saw me do this out of the corner of his eye. 'What are you doing?' he asked. 'Don't tear the bag! You are supposed to put the entire bag in the cup with the string hanging out on the rim of the cup.' He had also ordered a cup of tea and demonstrated how to place the tea bag into the cup filled with hot water. He then had the waitress bring another cup of hot water and tea bag for me.

"For my second attempt, I put the whole tea bag in the cup of hot water and saw the color changing to that of brewed tea. *Wow these Americans, they always come up with innovative ideas*, I thought.

"After about five minutes, I put some milk in the cup and looked around for sugar cubes or a cup that held the sugar. I asked my brother while he continued to read his documents, distracted, even after my earlier blunder.

"'Oh, the two small packets on the table are the sugar,' he said. While my brother kept on reading his files, I took the two packets of sugar while chuckling to myself and playfully threw them into the cup of tea. It was that way with the teabags, after all: why shouldn't it be the same with the sugar?

"It was at this point that Father Callistus put down the paperwork, started laughing, and playfully admonished me. 'You dummy, you have to tear open the sugar packets first before you put it in the tea.' At this, I just threw my arms up in frustration."

After recounting this story to me, my dad started laughing uncontrollably; he had to remove his glasses to wipe the tears. My mom also joined the laughter. I think my mom had heard this story a few times before, but she started laughing because she wanted me to join in. I just smiled.

"See, that *was* funny," he said to me, while continuing to laugh loudly.

"Yes, that was pretty funny," was all I could say. I all but fled and went to join my brothers watching TV, a little worried that I would have to listen to another one. It made his day to see me enjoy his story.

I could never tell a story like my dad or laugh as heartily as he could. As I got older, I always enjoyed listening to his stories and seeing him laugh. I just wished I had been a little more vocal in telling him just how I really felt about them.

Summer had finally come to Chicago, and my dad was happy that we were adjusting to our new surroundings incredibly well. He worked hard that year, and one day he came home in a happy mood, saying that he'd gotten a raise at work and that we were going to buy a car. I really wanted to go with them when they bought the car, but my parents told me that I had to watch my brothers while they went car shopping because they were not going to drag all three of us to the car dealer.

So it was that one Saturday afternoon my parents came back with a brand new car. It was a 1970, forest green Volvo 242. My dad explained to me that the "242" stood for two doors and four cylinders. I asked him what the second "2" stood for, but he said he did not know, and then immediately went on to explain to me all the features of this car in detail.

My brother James asked him why he got such an ugly, square car and I could see my dad getting angry and defensive because he read a similar question on my face. I thought it was a little boxy also: not like the sports cars that I had seen and thought he was going to bring home. My mom told us that it was actually an expensive car, and my dad added that it was the safest car around; it had been made in Sweden.

Eventually, I came around to really liking that car, especially after I got a chance to sit in the front seat when my dad and I went shopping together. My dad loved to drive and always loved the smell and shine of new cars. Throughout his life, unlike many of his Indian friends in the US, he would trade up for a new car every four to five years, whether he really needed one or not. He also loved to talk about his latest purchase to anyone who would listen, explaining why his newest car was the best.

Over the next few years we drove that boxy Volvo to many places around the city. Dad showed us downtown Chicago, the Fulton fish market, Maxwell Street market, and the Brookfield Zoo. We were finally able to really see Chicago beyond our little neighborhood.

He also took us to the Chicago lakefront, and we saw Lake Michigan up close for the first time, which was incredible. I couldn't believe how big it was. I never thought lakes could be big enough that you couldn't see across them. My dad mentioned that Lake Michigan was one of the five Great Lakes, and it was not even the biggest. We went to the lakefront frequently because my dad played volleyball with his Indian friends.

Unfortunately, there weren't too many other kids our age at the park.

It didn't matter, because the three of us always had fun running up and down Montrose Hill, which was situated at the center of the park. It was actually a large mound, but we loved laying sideways and rolling down it. That summer I fell in love with everything I saw of Chicago.

One of the most comical outings we had as a family was when my dad decided that we were all going to go see our first American film together at a nearby movie theater. My dad really wanted to take us to a movie, and this ended being up one of the strangest experiences of my early childhood.

My dad did not know a whole lot about western movies, but there we were one afternoon, in our seats at a nearby movie theater to watch a double feature.

Double features were a thing in the early seventies, and I'm sure my dad thought it was good deal to see two movies for the price of one. The double feature that day was a recently-released movie called *Butterflies are Free*, starring Goldie Hawn, followed by *The Graduate*, which was a movie that had been released a few years earlier.

The first movie with Goldie Hawn was an engaging story about a young blind man going out on his own against his mother's wishes to live in an apartment in the city. A young Goldie Hawn was his neighbor, and they eventually had a romantic relationship. It was a good story which I liked. In addition to the decent story, I also thought Goldie Hawn was beautiful, and she wore some skimpy outfits.

I was enjoying the movie and watching Goldie Hawn, but I did notice my mom glaring at my dad when Goldie Hawn was prancing around in the young man's apartment in a skimpy bikini. I could hear my dad whispering in her ear to reassure her. "This is the way young ladies dress in the US in the summer," he said.

My mom calmed down after a few more minutes of hushed conversation with my dad. I can now see why she reacted so strongly, since even kissing scenes back in those days were prohibited in the movies we saw back in India.

The first movie ended, and during the intermission we went to the lobby, where my dad bought us some peanuts and Coke before the second feature started. My brothers looked absolutely bored with the movie, so they were glad to get out to eat and drink. They wanted to go home, and my mom was also interested in leaving, but my dad insisted on us seeing both movies. He was going to get his money's worth. I asked my dad what the second movie was about.

"It's called *The Graduate*, but I'm not sure exactly what it's about. The movie is a few years old, but it won many awards."

I was not especially happy about this, because any award-winning movies that I saw in India were usually boring.

We settled back into our seats and *The Graduate* started. This one had some songs in it, which I liked, but it started to get boring. I was just about to fall asleep when all of a sudden the large screen was filled with Mrs. Robinson, the mother of the lead actor's fiancé, in her birthday suit. It was only for an instant, but I certainly never saw anything like that in Indian theaters before. My mom also saw it, and she stared daggers at Dad.

"Is this also how people dress in the US in the summer?" she whispered harshly. My mom quickly rounded the three of us up and marched us out of the theater, absolutely fuming. My dad sheepishly followed behind us.

During the ride home, my dad tried to explain to my mom that he did not realize the subject matter was not suitable for little kids, but my mom was still angry. The rating system was not as well defined as it is now in the movie industry.

It took a few days for things to get back to normal, but that was the last movie we went to as a family during my childhood. As a matter of fact, the subject of going to a double feature never came up again.

CHAPTER 9

THREE LITTLE EGGHEADS

"Three Little Eggheads"

It was Sunday afternoon, and my brothers and I were lined up along our small kitchen counter to get our haircuts. My dad was the family barber, and he wielded his electric hair clippers in one hand and a silver pair of scissors in the other like a gladiator going into battle. I remember the small case with all the adapters and equipment sitting on the end of the kitchen counter. My dad always cradled it like a valuable piece of art.

My brothers had finished their monthly appointment in the chair and come out with their heads looking like a lawn mower had run over it. As I walked up to the chair, I attempted to suggest a new arrangement.

"I'm twelve years old now. Why can't I have a haircut with a real barber?"

Dad tensed his lips and peered angrily through his glasses. "Those guys are expensive; and besides, I know how to give you boys good, clean haircuts." My mom and dad were frugal in those early years growing up in Chicago, since they were trying to get established in a new country.

I couldn't help but think to myself, *Jeez it's only a couple of dollars for a haircut; what's the big deal?*

Dad was not really taking any more of my questions, so I sat in the chair and waited for him to mangle my head. He had the same routine every time. After putting the scissors back in the case, he would start with the electric clippers and take a few long, sweeping swipes at the top of the head. He would then move to the sides with a closer rake setting.

After completing the rough first pass with the clippers, he would pull the shiny, silver scissors out from the case and make a few passes, snipping away over my entire head. I don't think he was doing any major cutting, but the echoes of those scissors clanking away still ring in my ears.

Finally, he would move onto his trademark feature, which was the half-circle over the ears. I absolutely hated this, because it never turned out anything close to a half-circle. It looked more like a meandering river that had nowhere to go. He would then take a glowing look at his accomplishment and proclaim his success.

"There you go. It's as good as what you can get at the barber, and we just saved five dollars." He was usually done with the three of us in under an hour and was always proud that he could do all three of us quickly. He always kept our hair short, because this was the easiest way to maintain it.

One day after he was done and feeling in a playful mood, he branded us the Three Little Eggheads. It was a name that stuck because it became a part of our vocabulary. If we were unhappy with one another, we would say, "You are such an egghead." My youngest brother got the brunt of the "Egghead" calling, because he was the youngest and was reluctant to give it back to his older siblings.

These days, I don't see my brothers often. My brother James lives in

California, so we may see each other once every few years. Even though my brother Joe is nearby, our family commitments and jobs always seem in the way of getting together more often.

When we were younger, even with the egghead haircuts, the three of us were inseparable, and we always managed to have a good time when we were together. We had our share of arguments, and even fights, but sports and music always seemed to save the day. The three of us were two and half years apart from each other, so we always had something in common to do.

As the oldest, my parents leaned on me to take care of my little brothers while they both went to work. I always tried to take care of my brothers, but I also took advantage of situations. My middle brother, James, didn't like the fact that I was always telling him what to do, so we occasionally clashed.

One thing that I hated was when he chose to become a Boston Bruins hockey fan instead of the family's beloved Chicago Blackhawks. To be fair, Boston usually had the better players and were the tougher team to beat back then, but I just could not understand why James would root for the Bruins.

To rub salt on the wound, he would make fun of the Blackhawks whenever the Bruins and Hawks played. I would always get worked up when our two teams got together, and unfortunately the Bruins always came out on top. James would always have this grin on his face as he gloated another Bruin victory over the Hawks, which would leave me fuming inside even though I did not express my frustrations readily.

My little brother Joe was the baby of the family, so I watched over him a little closer when my parents were not around. His disposition was similar to mine, so we always got along. I'm sure he looked up to his oldest brother, since I was five years older than he was.

I can still remember those care-free days when the three of us would walk back from our grade school, St. Boniface. We were really in no hurry to get home because once we got there, we had to finish our homework before going out to play. We took our time getting home, playing games on the sidewalk and talking away, dragging out the commute to avoid having to hit the books as long as we could.

All of us knew a lot about cars, so we made up games about determining what year any parked car was built during our walk home. We found out from our neighbor that the year of manufacture of a car was printed on the taillights, so we could confirm if our answers were correct. It was rare that we would miss on the year and make of the car, and when we did we knew we had stumbled onto a unique automobile. We would then discuss our find at length. My brother James, however, would ask me the same question over and over again as we passed by a nice-looking car: "Hey George, does that car cost more than ours?"

I'm not sure why he always asked this, but I think my dad convinced him that the Volvo we had was a good car at the time, and it was relatively costly, so he wanted to compare.

"I don't know; why do you keep asking about that?" I asked him.

"I just want to know," he would say and simply repeat his question.

He would also ask that very question to my dad when we were all in the car together, and my dad thought this was the funniest thing. He would crack up in laughter.

Even years later, whenever we spoke of James he would come out and reminisce with a chuckle. "Hey George, does that car cost more than ours?" He would then get tears in his eyes from laughter as he removed his glasses to wipe them off.

One of the stops we always made on our way back from school was the Augusta Bakery. It was about halfway on our trip home and situated on the corner of Ashland and Chestnut. We could smell the heavenly aroma permeating the air as we got closer. Our mouths would water when we saw the bakery in our sights. Our slow stroll would quickly transition into a flat-out sprint. We would line up against the picture windows to look at all the great pastries that were put on display.

One day, a lady who worked there came out and asked if we would like to try some. My brothers were eager to take up her offer as they headed into the store, but I stepped in to stop them.

"We don't have any money," I confessed.

"No, not what is displayed in the windows, but I have some donuts in back that I can give you," she offered. She took us to the rear of the store and gave us each a donut with chocolate icing on top. She explained to me that they throw away the ones that did not sell during the day. She assured us that they were still good, because they were made fresh in the morning.

She seemed like a lady who would not lie to us, so I thought it over and decided that my brothers and I would take her up on the free donuts. She also mentioned that if we stopped by after school on the days she worked, she would be able to give us some again. We nodded our heads and ate the donuts she gave us.

"Now, don't tell anyone else in school; otherwise, you boys won't have any left to eat," she cautioned as we left. Walking away with our mouths full and chocolate icing across our chins, we assured her we wouldn't tell anyone.

We were there every day on our walk back from school, and even though we kept our mouths shut about the free donuts, other kids started to show up too. We didn't always get free donuts, but if we lucked out with the right lady working there, she would take pity on the three of us and give us something for our walk home.

We decided not to tell my mom about the free treats, fearing that she would shut the door on our little treasure chest immediately. She wasn't completely unaware though; she began to question us on many occasions as to why we were not hungry at dinnertime.

After my mom started working, we had the apartment all to ourselves once we got home from school. Our parents told us that we could not leave the premises until either Mom or Dad got home, so we were stuck in our house or in the side yard. But we had no shortage of things to do. From making up games in the yard to watching all our favorite TV programs, we always kept busy. Of course, we had to get a good start on our homework, but we did the minimum needed in the afternoon and saved most of it for after dinner.

One of the games we routinely played, especially in the winter or on days when it rained in the summer was 'running bases'. This is a game normally played outside, but that didn't stop us. When it was too cold, raining, or hot outside, we could bring the game inside and still have loads of fun. Our living room, dining room, and kitchen were in a straight line, so we had just enough room to set up inside the house.

The game involved two guys throwing a ball back and forth from an agreed-upon distance, and the third person trying to run from one base to the other before the person catching the ball could tag their body with the ball and glove intact. If the throw was good, your only chance to get to the base was if you slid in just like the real baseball players do.

The single step from the living room to the dining room always kept things interesting when running from one base to another. Our living room carpet took the brunt of our slides, and my dad could never figure out why there was a bald spot on the rug right near the front coffee table.

Naturally, there were a couple of instances where we broke things and the game came to a complete halt. Once, when James's errant throw broke one of my dad's prized table lamps, things got really hairy. The lamp had a circular glass case that housed the light bulb, which sat on a golden Greek figure. As the ball struck the lamp, the lamp was catapulted from the table and landed with a shocking *crack* on the wooden coffee table in the living room. The glass case shattered into a million pieces and flew everywhere. We cleaned up as much as we could, but I think our mom found glass pieces all over the living room carpet days after the incident.

My dad was so mad that day when he came home that he had his belt out right away. We told him about playing 'running bases' inside, but we would not say who broke the lamp, so he gave us all a couple of lashes just so we wouldn't do it again. I always got the harder ones because I was the oldest, and he claimed that I should know better.

That night, I was yelling at James for breaking the lamp, and because I got hit with the belt the hardest.

"Hey, I got hit too," James yelled back.

"Me too," added Joseph, but we all knew that my dad only did it for show when he pretended to hit my little brother. Actually, he didn't really hit any one of us that hard, but we always feared him taking out his belt. I always felt my dad had a soft spot for my youngest brother; probably because he had not seen him until he had turned four.

Of course, neither James nor I would ever admit to doing anything wrong; he claimed his throw was not that bad and I should've caught it. I was about to pound him on his bed, but thought better of it in case Dad came back again with the belt.

That evening we received our sentence. We were grounded to our room for the weekend when not doing our homework or eating. Dad also made it clear that running bases was not allowed in the house anymore, or the consequences would be dire.

Our bedroom was about the size of a medium closet with two beds, so it was not all that much fun. There was a dresser in between the beds, under the window that overlooked our neighbor's window directly next to us. Only a narrow footpath was between the two buildings. Times like that, where we were mad at each other, made it hard for all three of us to be cooped up in our small bedroom, but we always made the best of it.

We didn't play running bases inside the house for a few months, but we picked it up again: this time with a homemade ball of paper and tape that did less damage to the furniture.

Once Mom or Dad came home from work, we were quick to go outside and play in our yard or at our friend's house across the alley. In the neighbor's house to the left of us across from our yard, there was a boy my age named Johnny. He didn't always play with us, but after a few years we were much closer and would always play.

During the summers when our parents were at work, he couldn't leave the house either, so he would always prop himself up on the high, gray-blue fence that separated our two yards. We found out he was Polish, which was not that unusual in Chicago; Chicago held the second-largest Polish population after Warsaw. I also found out that our landlady was Polish and the whole neighborhood was filled with many Polish families. I managed to pick up a couple of Polish phrases from Johnny and his mom, who always yelled out in her thick Polish accent, "Jasio, you need to get home right away." His parents were strict, and they weren't all that talkative.

My brothers James, Joseph, and I (left to right). In the background is our neighbor Johnny's house and the gray fence where his brother Rafal held court

One of the more interesting characters in the neighborhood was Johnny's older brother, Rafal. He was quite a bit older than the rest of us, but he always spoke with us to shower his wisdom on his brother and the three of us while we gathered by the corner of the fence next to the building that separated our two houses. He was probably ten years older than me, and he was tall enough that his head and shoulders always stuck out of the corner of his house as he draped his muscular arms over the fence to see us standing in our yard. He had long, slick-backed blond hair, and he always looked cool. Thinking back now, he was essentially the Polish Fonzie, the ultra-cool character of the day for young boys from the sitcom *Happy Days*.

We spent many late afternoons conversing with Rafal and his brother Johnny. In our eyes, Rafal knew everything. He taught my brothers and me about many things. He knew all there was to know about cars, movies, and the latest recording technologies. Cars from the fifties were his passion, and he would always talk about getting a powder blue '57 Cadillac convertible someday. He was also a movie and video buff and he owned several copies of reel-to-reel tapes of movies from the day. I never knew where he got all this equipment, but every so often he would allow us to come in and watch a movie.

I distinctly remember my brothers and I watching a segment of the movie *The Creature from the Black Lagoon* on a screen set-up Rafal had. It was just like going to the movies, which we never got to do after the aforementioned *Graduate* fiasco.

One of our cousins acquired our old house after we moved out, and they told me that Rafal continued to live in his parents' house for many more years; however, they sold the house to another buyer and my family lost track of them. I can still see Rafal sticking his head out from the top of the gray fence talking about his dream car, the powder blue '57 Cadillac. I hope he finally got one.

CHAPTER 10

YOUTHFUL EXUBERANCE

70's Fashion on display during a road trip—I can't believe I actually bought that shirt!

"Hold on; it's just around the corner," I yelled out to both Gina and Matthew in the back seat. On the way back from an afternoon Blackhawks game, I decided to drive north on Ashland Avenue instead of taking the Kennedy Expressway back to our home in the suburbs so that I could show my kids where their dad first grew up in the US.

After turning left on Augusta Boulevard from Ashland Avenue, we approached the alley a few blocks from our first apartment where we used to play with our neighborhood friends. I took a quick right, and then a left into the alley from Hermitage Avenue.

"What kind of street is this, Dad?" asked Matthew from the back seat.

"It's not a street; it's an alley," I answered. The city was configured in such a way that in between the streets, facing the back of homes, there were alleys. Chicago has an extensive network of alleys, and it's one of the most under-appreciated features the city has to offer. The alley may be unlovely, but it keeps the street fronts nice and clean because all the garbage pick-up takes place in the alley.

My brothers and I spent a lot of time in this particular alley, which was behind Augusta Boulevard in between Hermitage and Wood Street where we lived. Things had changed dramatically in thirty years, and I could not recognize many of the homes anymore because the yuppies had moved in, and teardowns were the norm.

The alley itself hadn't changed much since my early days when my brothers and I would walk there from our house. We would meet our neighborhood friends there to figure out what game we were going to play first. Street hockey, Nerf football, three bases, basketball, weightlifting, and a host of other games were always on the docket.

Each of us took turns daily selecting the game we were going to play. I usually chose hockey, especially in the winter, and I can still vividly remember stickhandling down the middle of the alley trying to avoid my friends on the opposing team and the huge, uneven cracks on the surface so that I wouldn't fall flat on my face.

Ever since that first encounter with Jimmy a month after we arrived in Chicago, the three of us were regulars at our neighborhood friend's house. In the summer months, we always met at Jimmy's house as soon as my mom or dad got home. Many of the neighborhood kids from nearby also joined us. If we had enough players, we would play football in the alley with a nerf ball. I always remembered the colorful array of names that were gathered.

Memo was Jimmy's brother, and he was in my brother James's grade, but you would never tell that by looking at him. He was twice the size of

James, but he was slow, speed-wise, when he was younger.

Then there was Enak, a tall, lanky kid from exactly where we did not know. But once or twice a week he would just show up. We were never able to pin down where he lived, but he was a good kid. He was not great at catching a football, but he could run. He would always go out for a bomb dashing into the makeshift alley end zone first. I usually got the ball to him, but it always slipped away from his fingers. One can always hear the groan of his teammates far away, yelling, "Eeeenak!"

There was also Rico from two doors down from Jimmy's house, who didn't have an athletic bone in him, but we let him play with us anyway because we needed bodies.

We never had the greatest equipment, and our "football field" was torn up with huge cracks and bumps, so that if you were not aware of the concrete ahead of you, you could fall flat on your face. This was the arena where I honed my limited athletic skills.

We played every sport available to us, from weightlifting on the second floor of Jimmy's garage (which was used for storage), to street hockey in the alley behind his house. In addition, we came up with games like "three bases," a version of baseball derived because of the limited space in Jimmy's dirt backyard.

Three bases was a game we played often, especially in the summertime when baseball was in full swing. The game consisted of a batter (without a bat) that took a baseball-sized rubber ball and threw it against a piece of wood that Jimmy's dad had nailed to the back of their garage. The field of play was the small, square dirt yard that stood between the house and the garage. The bases were arranged in a triangle, with the point of the triangle closest to the batter as home base.

Jimmy's house was sandwiched between two neighboring houses that had fences in their backyards. The houses themselves were separated by only a narrow walking path. First base was at the right side of home plate and second base on the left. Fielders consisted of a first baseman that covered first base, a middle infielder, and a shortstop that covered the left side.

By strategically throwing the ball at the wood, it would bounce off and send it either to the right side or left side. As soon as you hit the wood, the batter took off for first. Just like baseball, the fielders had to throw him out prior to the batter reaching first base. If the ball got past the fielder and escaped into the walkway clean without touching the fielder, then it was a home run. You also could not hit the ball in the air so that it hit the back of the house behind the fielders on the fly; if it did, the batter was immediately out. This was an important rule, because the windows of the building were about five feet above ground, and this kept the ball from breaking any windows.

I was amazed how much fun it was. It mimicked many of the attributes of baseball in a small space. I sharpened my fielding skills during these fun-filled games in the summer playing shortstop.

In the wintertime we usually played street hockey. It was my favorite game, and I started getting really good at it. Again, most of our equipment was either from the secondhand sports stores, or, as was the case for our goalie equipment, it was all homemade. We made cardboard goalie masks that were colored in to look like masks of our favorite goalies in the NHL, like Tony Esposito from the Blackhawks or Gerry Cheevers from the Boston Bruins. We would fold the thick cardboard in half and use a rubber band inserted at the ends of the mask to hold it in place.

Goalie leg pads were made from the foam torn from couch cushions that were put out for garbage. These would be tied to the goalie's leg near the upper calf and the ankle to hold it in place. Since the store-bought equipment was expensive, we became good at jury-rigging hockey equipment out of the most ordinary things that people chose to throw away.

The goalies were happy to get *any* kind of protection, as they were frequently exposed to Jimmy or I running down the alley on a breakaway, firing high, wicked wrist shots at the net. The hockey pucks we used were the plastic street pucks, but they were weighted down with pennies, through a slit we made on the side of the puck, to get better control while stickhandling.

The games got very competitive and, just like in the NHL, at times someone would get checked hard into the fences bordering the back of the neighborhood homes. Jimmy's brother Memo was a big kid, and one time he got carried away: he almost checked my brother James right through the fence. The wooden fence yielded and was almost parallel to the ground. James scrambled back up, unhurt, but the fence came back up only partially. The posts holding up the fence had cracked near the ground. It was not completely broken, but it looked bad.

We scattered and went into Jimmy's house, which was the closest to the alley, fearing that the neighbor would come out and find out that we ruined his fence. It is safe to say that we did not play hockey for a while after this incident.

A few weeks later, the fence was once again secure, but we made sure that we were careful not to have too many body checks against that fence. The neighbor was nice enough to repair the fence and allowed us to continue to play hockey.

After a few years in the area, I was able to get the lay of our neighborhood. I frequently had to go to the neighborhood stores to get something for my mom or dad, and because I was the oldest, I always ended up with this duty. It wasn't bad, because I always managed to convince my mom or dad to let me get a candy bar or a bag of potato chips while there.

There were two stores near our home that I frequented. One was a general store named Clara's, which was the closest to the house. Clara was an older lady that didn't always have much to say (at least to children), but she was always nice to me when I went in. The other one was two blocks away, and it was a general store and deli called Lattie's. I remember buying a lot of bologna, which was our favorite sandwich meat, from Lattie's. It was also cheap, so it was easy to convince Mom and Dad to get it for us. Thinking back on it now, I'm not sure how healthy it was for us, but it was a childhood staple for kids back in those days.

The deli was on the corner of Hermitage and Augusta. There were no 7-Eleven's around us in the early seventies, so the neighborhood was dotted with these small mom-and-pop shops. Both stores were small, especially Clara's store, which was no more than the size of an oversized closet. My dad was a smoker back in those days, so most of my visits to Clara's were to get cigarettes for him. His brand was Lucky Strike, but soon I was familiar with all the brands including Kent, Marlboro, and others.

My mom had always told me that I was never to smoke cigarettes, even though my dad smoked regularly and there were advertisements on TV for cigarettes every ten minutes.

I did get curious one day about smoking, so I rolled up a piece of ruled notebook paper to about the size of a normal cigarette and lit it in the bathroom when my parents were out one afternoon. I held it in my hands just like I saw the Marlboro man on TV and took a puff.

The inside of the rolled-up paper was still hollow, so the hot smoke went right into my throat and I coughed viciously as the homemade cigarette fell out of my hands. I was able to step on it quickly before it did any damage. I kept the bathroom fan on for five minutes and flushed the roll of paper (burned at the end) down the toilet before I stepped out. My brothers saw me come out and James asked why the bathroom smelled of smoke.

"It was probably from the fan overheating," I answered hastily. He gave me a puzzled look. I just walked away, not wanting to converse with him on this topic anymore. To this day I'm not sure if he knew what I was doing, but luckily for me he didn't mention anything to me or my parents.

I was lucky I hadn't hurt myself or burned down the bathroom that day, but if one good thing came out of that incident it was that I never wanted to smoke a cigarette ever again, and I never did.

On many weekend evenings, we would go out to one of my dad's Indian friends that lived in Chicago. Over the years many other families emigrated from our home state back in India, and we assembled in each other's houses for company.

These gatherings always had great food, and my brothers and I always had someone to play with during the evenings. The parties would continue late into the night, since my dad and his friends loved to play cards. They played Indian-style poker and I found out over the years that my dad was a good card player.

As us children played in a nearby bedroom, we could hear laughter and shouting coming from the card table. I was able to pick out my dad's voice. I found out from my uncles (as we affectionately called all his friends) that my dad would always be the one commenting on the game, or any other topic that he chose to talk about, usually to distract the other players so that he could win.

They didn't say it in so many words, but my dad was not only a good card player: his real secret was that he was a notorious trash talker at the poker table. I always wondered what kind of money was at stake during these games, and found out from my mom that she was not sure, but it seemed like Dad always came out ahead. One morning after one of these parties, I asked him how much money he made.

"I made enough for groceries this week," he said with a laugh.

When summer came, we usually got a visit from Uncle Richard. He was one of my dad's closest American friends who lived nearby. He had been one of the men with the funny-looking hats who had come to meet us at the airport when we had first landed, and it was Uncle Richard who took us back from the airport when we arrived from India. He was a terrific guy. He had a real adventurous spirit and would usually come by unannounced, riding his bike to the house to chat with us. He got into a bad car accident a few years after we arrived, so he rode his bike everywhere during the summer.

He was a bachelor, so he had all the time in the world. My mom would always invite him to dinner, and he always accepted because he loved to eat Indian food. Uncle Richard was well-traveled and had galloped across Europe. He primarily focused on countries I never knew anything about like Romania, Liechtenstein, San Marino, and many others.

Later in his life, on one of his European pilgrimages he became severely ill and sadly ended up dying in a Romanian hospital.

Uncle Richard was a history teacher at Mather, a Chicago public school, and he would always tell us cool stories about the countries he visited and the people he met. I really enjoyed how he would not just tell us about the places that he visited, but also explain how he interacted with the people and learned about their customs and culture. He would always only focus on one country at a time, and would stay a minimum of a month to absorb the culture.

He also got me interested in collecting stamps, which he said was a way to travel the world without ever leaving your home. He was right. My parents were just starting out in America, so the only vacations we took were to neighboring states in the summer.

Soon after Uncle Richard inspired me to begin collecting, I had stamps from over a hundred countries, and I really believed this planted the seed for me to explore the world.

Uncle Richard would always plead with my dad to take him to India, but my dad seemed reluctant about doing this, since he would need constant care: the everyday conveniences that he was used to in America were not readily available in Kerala.

Uncle Richard would also take us to baseball games at Wrigley Field and get us ice cream afterwards. My brothers and I would get the biggest sundaes or the tallest milkshakes.

After these outings all three of us were usually sick to our stomachs because we had eaten a couple of hot dogs and all kinds of snacks at the ballpark, and then top it off with a sundae or milkshake that was bigger than us on the way home.

James would tell my dad that Uncle Richard was kind to us and would buy us ice cream and a coke, unlike Dad (hint hint). I think my dad was a little put-out by this comment, and after this my dad nicknamed Uncle Richard, somewhat mockingly, "The Kind Man."

CHAPTER 11

MAESTRO

First home-cooked Thanksgiving meal, pictured here with my mom and brother James
in the back, and me and Joseph (right to left) in the front—November 1972

I recently visited my mom at the senior center near our home where
she is currently happily residing to discuss this book. Before I could
even start, I had to give her a quick status on our two children. She then
told me about all the activities she was participating in at the center.
Even now, in her eighties, she flips from bingo, painting, and flower
arrangement to knitting, usually heading up many of these activities.

While walking around the center, she always introduced me to
everyone she had befriended in the short time that she was there. This
was apparently everyone we crossed paths with; that's just who she was.
She still seems to have limitless energy, and can adapt to any situation and

make the best of it. Initially it was very tough on her when Dad passed away, but she found the energy to live her life again.

Finally, after our obligatory cup of afternoon tea, I started quizzing her about her first job. I asked her if she was scared when she took the job after only a few short years of being in the US. She recounted that she had not been afraid at all; she adapted quickly, and everyone liked her.

In my eyes, Mom had no fear. She took on anything, and in every situation she figured out a way to succeed. My dad was the dreamer, always thinking about the future, but my mom solved all the daily problems. I always appreciated her simple and direct approaches to finding creative solutions to everyday challenges. She continues to be a wonderful role model to me on assimilating to new situations with flexibility, intelligence, and determination.

I asked Mom about the old days back in Chicago as well, and she obliged with more stories.

After my dad got his new car, he would drop my mom off at her workplace in downtown Chicago. It was about a thirty-minute ride from our home, and the three of us usually rode in the car with Dad and Mom. On the way back, my dad would drop us off at our school.

My dad was really into music, both Indian and English, so there would always be tunes bursting out of the radio of our green Volvo, which was tuned to WLS AM radio. It was rare to have FM in a car radio in the early seventies, so AM was all we had.

Larry Lujack was my dad's favorite disc jockey back then, and he would always be commenting on Lujack's musings for that morning. Lujack would also play hit songs to keep us entertained during the ride. One of the most vivid memories I have of being in the car is of my dad trying to sing the then-current "Top Forty" English songs. From singing along to "Papa Was a Rollin' Stone" to belting out the exaggerated, high-pitched "Maaaaurice" from Steve Miller's hit "The Joker," it was always entertaining.

From an early age, I was exposed to all kinds of music. My dad would play Indian music at home, and whenever we rode around the car the radio would be on, playing the current hits. No matter what language or genre, music would move him. He was also a good singer, and at home and in the car, he would belt out a tune with his own special blend of emotion.

One of the traditions in our house when we got a little older was to allow the three of us to choose an English album to play every Friday night on his nice music system, which included a receiver, a turntable, and even a cassette deck. My brothers and I would choose the loudest rock 'n' roll album that we had, but he would patiently listen to the whole album with us. There would be lots of commentary from him, but he would stick with it until the end. My brothers and I would look forward to these listening sessions every Friday evening.

Mom didn't necessarily love music, but she enjoyed when my dad and the three of us were listening to music together. She seemed happy when we were together. She was never one to sit still and be patient enough to listen to music for too long, because she had too many other tasks that needed to be completed.

There were few moments that my mom outwardly showed any sign that she was not feeling well or that something was wrong. She was always on the go and kept everyone on their toes.

My mom worked extremely hard all her life, both in her job in downtown Chicago and taking care of her family at home. She worked at Carter & Holmes, a company that distributed ties to many of the great Chicago-based upscale department stores of the time, like Marshall Field & Co, Saks Fifth Avenue, and Lord and Taylor. Her building was at the end of the Ohio Street Extension ramp that takes you from the Kennedy Expressway to downtown Chicago.

I can still remember the Ohio Street exit ramp rising above us as we drove towards my mom's building. There was always a spectacular view of the city and its iconic buildings as we approached Orleans Street. Heading east, it was easy to spot the many skyscrapers and other unique buildings of Chicago.

The enormous Merchandise Mart building could be seen on the right, and on the left side was a building with a pitch-black water tower. The L-train running over Franklin Street, packed with commuters, was a common sight directly in front of us as we approached her building, which rose above on our left side on the corner of Ohio and Orleans.

I still get a thrill driving into the city taking the Ohio Street ramp from the Kennedy because the elevated view over the years has only gotten better. Seeing Mom's building (which is still standing) and the elevated Franklin Street L-line always brings back fond memories of me as a kid going with my dad and brothers to drop off my mom at work in our green Volvo.

We went inside one day to see her workplace, and it was fun seeing all of the ties lined up for inspection. My mom gave us a little overview of her responsibilities and introduced us to all her colleagues and supervisors. They all had very positive things to say about Mom, and I felt proud.

My mom talked glowingly about Carter & Holmes, and she loved working there. When I was a little older I was also able to go into her work and select the best ties for a discounted price. As a young adult, I always had on the best ties.

My mom was not shy. She was confident in whatever she did, and tried to instill that same determination and confidence in the three of us. There were a few instances where we needed a fourth player so that we could play when our friends weren't around, and my mom was the first one to step in. She had complete confidence that whatever we were doing she could pick up quickly and participate. I admired her for her positive attitude and the pride she took in whatever she did.

As a kid, I liked the fact that my mom worked for Carter & Holmes because at Christmastime the company allowed the entire family to go to the circus at Medinah Temple, which was a few miles away from where she worked. Medinah Temple was located east of her workplace, closer to Lake Michigan.

Later in life, after conducting a little research I learned the reason why there was a mosque-like temple in the middle of downtown Chicago: the Chicago Shriners needed a meeting place and a convention center in the early 1900's, and the fraternal group's official name told the tale: The Ancient Arabic Order of Nobles of the Mystic Shrine.

Considered one of the grandest Shrine temples in the US, Medinah Temple opened in 1913 on the eastern half of a city block, bounded by Wabash, Ontario, State, and Ohio Streets. Even at my young age, it was easy to see that the surrounding modern skyscrapers struck a sharp contrast to the exotic, onion-shaped domes of Medinah Temple, but it did not seem out of place.

When we walked into the building for the very first Christmas event, I couldn't believe all the ornate carvings on the ceiling and the rich-colored walls of the lobby. The interior also featured a banquet hall with space for 2,300 patrons and a 4,200-seat auditorium featured a huge pipe organ. The inside looked cavernous with its high, domed ceilings.

The structure continues to amaze me whenever I drive by, and remains one of the country's finest examples of Middle Eastern-style architecture.

I also found out that the circus that we went to, sponsored by my mom's workplace, was indeed the Medinah Shrine Circus benefiting the Shriners philanthropies.

While at Medinah, we not only got a chance to see a great circus: all the children also received a nice Christmas gift. My brothers and I couldn't wait to tear into the presents that they gave us. It was usually a board game or a small Hot Wheels set, but we cherished it.

The most memorable gift I received was Rock'em Sock'em Robots.

This was a boxing game with bright blue and red plastic boxers that could be manipulated with manual hand controls. The head was on a spring mechanism, and if you can hit your opponent's chin just right the head would pop up and you would win. It was a game that would fail to get by the children's toy safety regulators now.

The Medinah temple of my childhood where I enjoyed the circus is now a Bloomingdales department store; thankfully, the exterior still looks the same. I have yet to go inside since it's been transformed, and I don't think I ever will. There are too many great memories of the way things once were, and I feel like they would be affected if I were to step into the place now that it's different than I remember. Maybe one of these days I will take my kids inside to show them where their dad and uncles went to the circus in the middle of the city. We may have to dig deep into our imaginations to see the circus once performed at a department store.

Even though my mom enjoyed working at Carter & Holmes, working downtown for her was also a struggle due to my dad's work schedule. She had to take the Grand Avenue bus back home every night. In the summer it wasn't so bad, but taking transit, followed by the long walk from the bus stop to our apartment (sometimes in freezing cold weather) was exhausting. It extended the usual thirty-minute trip by car to almost one and a half hours. On really cold days, I still remember her warming up by our heater for a good ten minutes.

One day I was giving my own kids, Gina and Matthew, a hard time about always giving them rides to their schools every morning. I let them know that during my day I had to walk almost a mile each way to my school. My mom was with me at the time, and this is where she stepped in.

"One mile, ha! I had to walk about two miles after work to get home because the stop nearest our apartment was a little too secluded; I was forced to get off the bus earlier, which meant that I had to walk even farther. There were days when it was so cold I had to enter stores and warm up before walking out again."

Mom and I at the rear of our apartment

This shut me up quick. After getting home there was no time to rest because she had to prepare dinner for the family and then make sure that the three of us did all our homework. Then it was time to get to sleep and be ready to do it all over again the next day.

I hadn't realized how hard she worked so that we could have a normal and enjoyable life in Chicago. Money was tight for them, but I always felt like we had enough. My mom was efficient at everything she did, and would always find a way to complete everything that she set out to do successfully. As an adult I noticed that I picked up some of these traits from my mom and I'm grateful, because it really helped me during my career at work.

Unlike my dad, my mom did not have the opportunity to attend college. She made up for it by having really good common sense and a determined work ethic.

Every Friday, the whole family usually went shopping on Chicago Ave. The now-extinct National Supermarket was a frequent stop to buy groceries as my mom planned out the meals to make for the upcoming week, balancing just how much we could spend.

My brothers and I always tried to convince her to buy junk food cereals like Coco Puffs and Count Chocula (two of our favorites), or classic Chicago snacks like Hostess cupcakes and Cherry pies, which were my favorite. I always managed to talk her into getting a few of these. She was firm about not eating too much junk food, but at the end of the shopping session we always got something.

On other days if we needed items for the house, we would go to nearby department stores: Goldblatts or Weiboldt's. Goldblatts, which is no longer in business, was one of the biggest regional stores in the Chicago area. The original building that we went to still stands to this day, but it is relegated to office space.

I also loved going to the Weiboldt's department store, which has also gone out of business. It was my dad's favorite store. The only reason I liked the store was because they offered green stamps with every purchase, which you saved in little books that could be redeemed for an array of merchandise. My mom would diligently collect and paste all the stamps, hoping to have enough so that she could get us something nice.

I remember looking through the catalogs and seeing the baseball gloves and hockey equipment that could be redeemed, but we never accumulated the needed amount of books to even get close to getting those items. In the end we always ended up with some cheesy decorative item for the house that my dad usually threw away after a few months.

Driving north down Ashland Avenue one day after attending a Blackhawks game, I pointed out a building to my kids that is currently a lawyer's office. "This used to be a clinic that my mom took me to for our regular checkups," I told them as we passed it. "I still get a shiver as I go by this place, because I was so afraid of doctors and getting injections."

Mom would take all three of us at once, and we would anxiously await our turn to have a nurse give us shots. Mom would take us as scheduled, and we would always ask her why we needed to be there. I remember she would try her best to calm us down as much as possible in the most patient way. Even though my mom and dad were new to this country and culture, they always took good care of us in what must have been stressful circumstances for them.

My mom was a good cook, especially when it came to Indian cooking. My brothers hated Indian food and would always want American food. My mom tried hard to cook meals like meatloaf, baked chicken, and other common American dinners, but I preferred her Indian meals. Her Indian cooking was much better than her American cooking.

James complained the loudest when it came to eating Indian food after he got a taste of the American diet. He was always campaigning for American takeout. These days I give my son Matthew a hard time and tell him that he is "just like his Uncle Jimmy" when he refuses to eat home-cooked Indian meals. Interestingly enough, as an adult James is probably the healthiest eater of the three of us.

All three of us hated vegetables when we were younger, and we usually gagged at the thought of eating steamed broccoli or cauliflower, which always seemed to be on the dinner table. I was willing to eat a little bit more if it was spiced up Indian style, but I'm sure my brothers didn't eat any vegetables except maybe for lettuce on their burgers and corn during a BBQ.

My mom was fairly tall for a South Indian woman, and she was athletic. She used to tell us stories of her high school days and her love for basketball. She claims she was good when she had the opportunity to play on the high school team.

My mom was definitely a better athlete than my dad, and it was usually my mom who was up for playing with us when we all went to the park as kids. Even in her seventies she was always up for a challenge when she was with her grandchildren. From jumping rope with my daughter to playing basketball with my son, she kept fit and active. I always thought she was exaggerating when she said she was a good basketball player, but after seeing her handle a ball and shoot, I'm convinced.

While growing up I took for granted what my mom did for us. We always expected her to be there whenever we needed anything. She was always by our side whenever we were in trouble, were sick, sad, or just plain bored. That's just who she is. Her family was and continues to be everything to her: always priority one.

I remember thinking when I was in college that my mom would have made a great CEO, because she had all the traits of a great leader: smarts, compassion, flexibility, strong work ethic, and the ability to get things done in tough situations. I was always happy that I had a mom that I learned from just by being with her day-to-day, and I firmly believe it made me a better leader in my adult life. Her leadership skills and compassion always shone through.

Looking back, both my parents had a real impact on me. I benefited from my mom's organization and leadership skills, and from my dad I got the love of music, travel, books, and the ability to dream big.

CHAPTER 12

FIRST SKYSCRAPER CONQUERED

The Prudential Building, Chicago

L ife at St. Boniface grade school began to settle in by the middle of
7th grade, and I finally felt like just another one of the students. I was
speaking English fluently and only a trace of my Indian accent remained.
I noticed that I no longer thought in my native tongue, and even though I
could understand it clearly, my speaking and writing abilities in Malayalam
were dwindling.

I had numerous friends, and I enjoyed all the activities that we did in
school. The only game I remember playing with my school friends outside
during recess was Midnight. We didn't have a playground, so the only
time we could play was when a section of the street was barricaded in the

morning and afternoon when we were entering and leaving the school. This left us with the width of the street next to the school as our playground.

The object of the game was pretty simple: just get to the other side of the street without getting tagged. I played sometimes, but it got boring quickly. Unfortunately, there were no other extra-curricular sports activities at our school. Usually I spent most of my time talking to anybody who would listen about the Blackhawks game the previous evening, or whether they wanted to play hockey over the weekend.

My friend Andrew was a big hockey fan, and he was always open to playing hockey on the weekends. I convinced my mom to allow me to walk to a school with a nice, tarred surface near his house where we could play. It was on the same route that we took to our school, so she let me go. My brothers didn't want to come with me because of the long walk, but I would take my street hockey stick and puck and would walk for about a half hour so that I could play with Andrew. Usually it was just him and me, so we switched off with one of us being a goalie and the other taking shots.

Andrew was a good friend during grade school, but he was a troublemaker at school. He was a smart kid and was always nice to me, but people misunderstood him because he liked to tease people. I normally disregarded his comments; I thought at times that he was pretty funny. He ended up going to high school with me, but I lost track of him when he was kicked out of school after the first year. His penchant for finding trouble only got worse in high school.

Fortunately for me, because we knew each other from grade school, he never directed his anger at me. I tried tracing him down later as an adult, but to no avail. I will always remember those sunny winters on Saturday afternoons playing one-on-one hockey with Andrew.

One of my favorite memories of my days at St. Boniface was our fieldtrip to downtown Chicago. The whole class was loaded into a school bus, which took us to the heart of the city near the lakefront. My dad had driven us downtown while dropping my mom off at work, but this was the first time that I would be spending time learning about the city and the incredible architecture that it had to offer.

In 7th grade I was not exactly interested in learning about great architecture, but I looked forward to the trip, and especially the opportunity to go up in a tall skyscraper. I found out that the focus of our trip was to go up on the very first skyscraper built in Chicago after the Great Depression.

After arriving at the Prudential Building, we all filed out of the bus and entered the lobby on the first floor. It looked incredibly busy with people moving around everywhere. Then Mrs. Diane, our 7th grade teacher, started telling us about the Prudential Building.

The Prudential Building is a forty-one-story structure in Chicago, completed in 1955 as the headquarters for Prudential's Mid-America company. It was the first skyscraper built in Chicago after the Great Depression of the 1930s and the Second World War.

When the Prudential building completed construction, it had the highest roof in Chicago. Its mast served as a broadcasting antenna for Chicago's WGN TV, which was one of our favorite stations. This was to be the first skyscraper in Chicago that would not need to have its windows cleaned from the outside: all its windows swung open vertically, allowing them to be washed from the inside.

Then she went on to say that another first for the building was the result of the decision to install escalators that would serve the building's top two floors. Installing the highest escalator system in the world (at the time) would allow the elimination of the "penthouse" normally used for housing elevator machinery at the top of the building, which would have been out-of-place for this modern skyscraper.

Mrs. Diane continued to give us the history on the building, which I found interesting in the beginning, but devolved into me getting extremely bored. Finally, someone yelled, "When are we going up?" The rest of us echoed the sentiment, and our teacher led the way.

We did finally go up to the viewing tower. First we took the longest escalator I had ever seen, and then the elevator. I had never taken an elevator for more than a couple of floors before, and as it went up packed with most of our class, I started feeling a little queasy. Luckily, I didn't have to throw up like Carolyn, one of the strangest classmates I had in grade school. She lived behind our house.

Carolyn was a girl that would always talk in class, but no one would listen to her. She even threw garbage in our backyard once and would tease me about it in school. I mostly ignored her.

After we got to the top, Mrs. Diane let us roam around, and I was awestruck by the view that the height provided. Chicago was laid out majestically on all four sides of the building. My favorite view was of the lakefront, from the north of the building, where the shoreline hugged Lake Michigan. Looking further up I could see the John Hancock building, which had been completed just a few years back. It towered over every other building, including ours.

As I stared at the building, I couldn't help but be overwhelmed at the thought of the individuals that had to get up every morning to construct that beautiful behemoth. Mrs. Diane told us that the name of the building was after one of the signatories of the declaration of Independence: the Hancock tower matched the boldness of his signature. The John Hancock building became my favorite skyscraper in Chicago from that day on.

CHAPTER 13

HOCKEY IN MY BLOOD

Bobby Hull, "The Golden Jet"

E ven though I didn't go see movies with my dad after the double feature incident, sports always brought my dad and I together. We were both extremely loyal to the Chicago teams, and our whole family watched games together, especially hockey. Throughout my life it did not matter how much my dad and I disagreed on other issues: when it came to hockey and the Chicago Blackhawks, we would always have a happy and lively discussion.

On a chilly spring day in 2019, my son Matthew and I were sitting in a sports bar on Taylor Street. We were in the Little Italy neighborhood getting a bite to eat before heading to the Blackhawks game we were slated to see. Usually every year we go to the game as a family, but this time only Matthew and I could make it. We both had our favorite Blackhawks jerseys on, and we were excited about watching the Blackhawks play live. It was his final year of high school, and it gave us a chance to spend some quality time together before he went off to college later in the year.

We talked a little bit about college and he was unusually attentive to what I had to say.

"Hey, are you a little nervous about going away to college?" I asked him.

He answered back as he was taking a bite out of his gargantuan cheeseburger. "No, not really. I'm not sure how it's going to be, so I guess I have a little anxiety about that. But I am looking forward to meeting new people, and to my engineering classes at Purdue."

I realized then that he was not afraid of new situations and would be just fine being on his own at college. Exchanges between the Maliekal men on serious topics such as these were usually quick, and Matthew was no different. If the same discussion were to occur with my daughter today, it would easily be over an hour of conversation. And if it was between my wife and my daughter, it could easily be two to three hours. But we simply went back to eating our cheeseburgers and commenting on the Duke basketball game we were watching. Such was the nature of our father-son relationship.

After finishing our meals and watching the basketball game at the sports bar for a short time, we headed to the United Center a few blocks away. As we walked by the sculpture depicting legends Stan Mikita and Bobby Hull, two great Chicago Blackhawks of the past, I could see by the look in his eyes that Matthew was feeling similar emotions to what I felt whenever I go to a Hawks game. I always got goosebumps walking up to the stadium entrance and then finally entering to see the cavernous facility with the ice rink below.

As I walked down Madison Avenue with my son that day, I couldn't help but drift back forty-five years to when I took the exact same strides on Madison Avenue with my dad.

My dad and I were on our way to see my first hockey game at the old Chicago Stadium, which was also my dad's first live game.

Our family became big hockey fans soon after we arrived from India. Growing up in the city, I lived and breathed the Chicago Blackhawks. I always wondered how my dad became a hockey fan, and as I got older I learned why. There weren't too many hockey fans from India, but fortunately for me, my dad and his roommates when he was a student (who he was now close friends with) were also hockey fans. Watching hockey was a fun way to pass the time during the cold Chicago winters when you only knew a few people.

In 1973, the Blackhawks made it to the Stanley Cup finals against the hated Montréal Canadiens, and my dad surprised me with an offer to take me to game three of the seven-game series at the Chicago stadium. I could not believe my luck. I had never been to a hockey game, and my first one was going to be a Stanley Cup final series matchup.

I only found this out later in life, but it turns out that one of my mom's bosses, Fred Kahn, who was a huge Blackhawks fan and season ticket holder, gave my mom two tickets due to the great work that she had done for him. They were standing room tickets, but I did not really care. I was not even sure what that meant at the time. All I knew was that I was going to see a Stanley Cup Finals game with my dad.

On game day, I was so excited that all I could talk about was the Blackhawks. My brother James was not too upset about not going, probably because he was (for some inexplicable reason) *not* a Blackhawks fan, even though he was a hockey fan.

As we approached the Chicago Stadium, I was overwhelmed at hearing all the excitement around the building. What a building it was. I could tell it was old, but its classic 1920's architecture looked magnificent against the western Chicago sky in the setting sun.

We walked to our special entrance, Gate 3 ½. It was at this time that my dad explained to me that we had standing room tickets, and that we would not be able to sit down during the entire game. I didn't care. I was so excited I told him that I could stand all night if I was watching the Blackhawks play at the Chicago stadium. I think the real reason he mentioned it to me was because *he* was a little worried about standing for the whole game.

Once inside, we made our way up to the third balcony standing room section after taking what seemed like five hundred steps on the never-ending set of stairs. My dad was so exhausted by the time we got to the top that he had to rest for a good ten minutes before we got to our perch to watch the game. We were high up, way in the back, but I could still see the ice surface as I watched the two teams doing their warm-up skates. In the background, the Blackhawks theme song "Here Come the Hawks" was playing. I sang along loudly, since I knew most of the song by heart. The Blackhawks were the only team to have a theme song back then, and it put me and the rest of the crowd in a jovial mood.

The players seemed distant, but it was such an improvement over watching the game on a nineteen-inch black and white TV back home that I didn't care if we had the absolute furthest view away from the ice surface. My young eyes worked perfectly, and I was able to make out all the numbers on players. I was mesmerized at seeing the Chicago Blackhawks in their white uniform with the legendary Indianhead on the chest.

As a kid, I spent hours trying to recreate that logo on paper. It was a rare sight to see the Blackhawks in their home uniform, which was white at the time. Back in that era of Chicago Blackhawks hockey, the owner of the Blackhawks, Arthur Wirtz, was so scared of upsetting his season ticketholders that he refused to show any of the home games on TV. Even more amazing, he didn't broadcast the first period of home games on the radio, fearing that he would upset the season ticketholders who were late to the game. Unbelievable!

This practice was not only the norm in Chicago for the regular season games, but also for the playoffs and the Stanley Cup finals. The only time that I saw the Blackhawks don their white home uniforms during the early seventies was from the highlights of the previous evenings' game on TV the next morning. The Chicago-based Ray Rayner show was my go-to source for all the sports scores and highlights; I'd watch it every morning at 7:15AM before making our way to school.

The game started, and after a few minutes everyone sat in their seats. I was now able to see clearly from our standing position. One of the gentlemen sitting in front of us invited me to stand on the steps near him so that I could get a better view of the ice surface.

The Hawks scored early, and there was a huge roar as everyone stood up to cheer them on. The noise was so loud that I thought my ears were going to pop. When the crowd got really going, I could feel the wooden planks of the old stadium under me sway in rhythm. It shook me to my core. I loved it. Everyone around me was high-fiving me and they all, my dad included, had this delirious look of happiness imprinted on their faces. I'm sure I looked the same.

During the first period break, my dad and I went to one of the food stands, and I remember the two of us standing near a counter as we ate our hot dogs. The hot dogs weren't that great, but it didn't matter. There was nothing that could spoil that night, and I went from looking at my dad to scanning the crowd walking by in the tight Chicago Stadium hallways with a huge smile on my face and a hot dog stuffed in my mouth.

The Hawks went on to win big, and after the game I had the biggest smile on my face as I looked up at my dad thankfully as we made our way home. It was a night that I would always remember, not just because I got a chance to see my Blackhawks beat the dreaded Canadiens in a

Stanley Cup game but because my dad had been there with me and we experienced it together.

After getting home, I wanted to tell my mom and brothers all about the game and what a great win it was. Unfortunately, my brothers were asleep and my mom told me that it was late and that I had to go to sleep. I was so wired that night it seemed like forever before I was able to sleep. All I could think about was how this was the best night of my life. It had been a long day for me also, and I was running on adrenaline. Finally, I drifted off to sleep.

Unfortunately, the Canadiens, led by Yvan Cournveyer and Ken Dryden, went on to defeat my beloved Blackhawks, and the Canadian team once again walked off with the Stanley Cup at the Chicago Stadium, just like they had two years prior.

The early seventies were the golden era for the Blackhawks, but even though they had one of the top teams they just could not capture the elusive Stanley Cup. It would be another thirty-seven years to wait until I saw the Blackhawks hoist a Stanley Cup: when they beat Philadelphia in 2010.

Many years after that game in 1973, I got a chance to meet at length with Bobby Hull, or the "Golden Jet" as he was known in Chicago. He got the nickname because Bobby Hull was one of the greatest hockey players to don skates, and he was unstoppable when he was rushing the length of the rink to unleash one of his lethal slap-shots at a hapless goalie.

It was at a work event at Ditka's restaurant in Chicago Downtown where he was our celebrity speaker after dinner. After the formal sessions of the evening, I had the chance to sit down with Bobby and have a glass of wine with the Golden Jet. I was forty years old at the time, but I'm sure my face displayed the same excitement I showed back in the early seventies watching him play.

We spoke about the 1971 Stanley Cup Game, where the Canadiens had also beat us; he was not happy thinking back to that game when I brought it up. This was the Stanley Cup Final series two years prior to the game I attended, which had also ended on a disappointing note.

I started off the conversation by saying, "Bobby, what happened in Game Seven of the Stanley Cup Finals in Chicago back in '71?"

He tensed up, clenching his enormous forearms, which looked like two small tree trunks sticking out of his tan-colored, checkered short-sleeve shirt. "What about that game?"

"Well, how did you guys lose that game? We were up 2-0 with the best goaltender in the league, Tony-O, and we lost 3-2."

"How do you know about that game? You look way too young."

"I was eleven years old at the time, and I was listening to broadcaster Lou Pettit, the best hockey announcer ever. He painted the action on the ice as I listened to the game on the radio."

"He was very good," agreed Bobby.

"I can still hear his call when you hit the post behind Ken Dryden in the last two minutes of the game! It would've been the tying goal."

"You don't have to tell me, young man. To this day, I still think about that third period," he said, and I could see by his expression that it was true.

By this time, he was pointing his finger in my face, getting more fervent as he recalled more. "But our coach, Billy Reay, decided to give two of our weaker players more ice time instead of putting me out there."

Bobby Hull was a passionate person, and he displayed his emotions on his sleeves whether he was on or off the ice. Someone actually took a photograph during our animated conversation that evening, and I have a framed picture of Bobby with his finger precariously close to my face, which I had turned away in a mixture of laughter and fear.

"We should've won that game. We were the better team!"

I wanted to discuss the details of the game I remembered a little more, but his face was flushing red, so I decided to back off; I didn't want our

Chicago Celebrity Representative to start ranting about his glory days in front of the many physicians that I had assembled for a work conference earlier in the day.

We moved on to another subject and finished our wine, and then we joined some of the other assembled guests. It was one of the more interesting conversations I had in my life: sharing with one of my childhood heroes my thoughts on a championship hockey game that I'd heard as a kid on the radio. We all know that another Chicago athlete, Michael Jordan, was extremely competitive, but I'm not sure he had anything on the "Golden Jet".

Unfortunately, there were some deep-seated problems that he had with the Chicago coach and the following year after the '71 season, the Blackhawks decided to let him go. Bobby jumped to the new hockey league that was forming, called the WHA, and signed the first million-dollar contract by a hockey player.

To my regret, I never got a chance to see him play live, since my first game was two years later, but I followed him on TV. He wasn't the global icon that Michael Jordan was, but everyone in Chicago knew the "Golden Jet" when he played for the Blackhawks. I would've loved to have been at the old Chicago stadium to see him wind up and skate from one end to the other, culminating in a 100MPH-plus slap-shot.

CHAPTER 14

"THE RAT ALWAYS GETS THE CHEESE"

The Graduate

During elementary school, I was an altar boy at St. Boniface and had to serve masses a couple of times a week. I was previously an altar boy in India, so I knew the routine. After the initial excitement of being an altar boy in the US, it became a little monotonous: in addition to going to mass every week with my parents, I had to attend one or two additional masses during the week.

I always enjoyed serving weddings and funerals because the families usually tipped us. I felt bad about getting money during someone's funeral, but I didn't refuse the money given to me at the time. One time I received ten dollars for a wedding, which was the most amount of money I'd ever had. I didn't tell my parents or my brothers about it and instead bought candy and hockey cards for two weeks straight.

Even as a young boy I enjoyed the challenge of participating in many activities, so I also became an assistant crossing guard near the school. We were referred to as "Patrol Boys." As dorky as that sounds now, that's what we were called. I remember asking my son one day when he was in grade school whether there were Patrol Boys in his school.

"What are you talking about, Dad?" he asked me. "We have adult crossing guards that do that; besides, everyone comes in a school bus."

Well, we didn't have buses at St. Boniface, and we only had one crossing guard, who needed helpers. Actually, the main reason I signed up was because of the cool, bright orange patrol belt that we received and proudly wore when we were at our station. I made sure every night that I folded up the belt just right so that I could display it prominently to let everyone know that I was a Patrol Boy.

We received about ten minutes of training on what to do and how to use our arms to help little kids cross the streets. Most of the kids didn't pay attention to us, but the little ones always thought we were pretty special and paid attention to everything we said.

I took my crossing duties seriously and was proud that I was there to make sure the younger kids crossed the streets safely. I thought I looked pretty cool at the time with my belt on. Of course, my kids were laughing so hard when I told them about being a Patrol Boy and wearing my orange patrol belt. Now that I think about it, I wonder why they entrusted 7th and 8th graders with crossing kids on busy streets. I can see why it wouldn't work today.

As I started 8th grade, I felt especially great when I found out that Mr. Alan Cichon would be teaching my grade. He had been my teacher in 6th grade, and even though he could be a bit of a disciplinarian, I really liked him. He was young, energetic, and had a real passion for educating children. He was also very hands-on: in addition to our daily class material, we were always working on various projects that gave us first-hand experience on the topics we were learning. I still remember when we were learning about world history, he helped put on an international night with many activities to participate in. We also brought a sampling of food from our native countries.

He was always pushing me to do better, and even though I still struggled a bit in English writing, he continued to encourage me to improve. His class was always well-behaved, and even though we had some troublemakers, he always seemed in control.

Mr. Cichon had a way of gaining the respect of all the students when he spoke. He never yelled, but rather chose his words carefully to get kids to listen. He was another great example for me to learn from. I'm not sure if I ever measured up to do as well as Mr. Cichon to persuade groups and individuals to achieve beyond what they think they can accomplish, but I strived to compare.

Early in the year I found out that the whole class would be going to Kenosha for an overnight stay at a camp. I was super excited until I got home and my dad told me that I could not go because he did not want me to stay away from home overnight. I tried to work on my mom to convince Dad, but he was not budging. It was not until Mr. Cichon called my parents to let them know that it would be all right and that since everyone was going, I would be missing a great experience if I didn't go. After the call, my dad finally conceded and let me go.

The ride to Kenosha, Wisconsin took about two hours, but for me it went very quickly. We were all happy to be on the bus laughing and talking up a storm. Everyone was thrilled to be together instead of back home doing schoolwork. This was a time for our small class to really bond, since the next year we would all be headed to high school, and some of us may never see each other again.

When we arrived at the camp, the eight boys were all in one big room with bunks for everyone. The dozen girls from our class were situated in two other rooms across from the huge great room. I tried to get a bed close to my friend Gary, since he was the guy I enjoyed talking to the most.

Over the past couple of years in grade school, Gary and I had become good friends. We enjoyed sports and would either play or talk about them all the time. I was frequently at Gary's house, where we would play on the basketball court at the grade school in front of his house. After our games, he would invite me to his house where he lived with his parents, his brother, and four sisters. The Sylvie household was always lively, and his family was always friendly to me. I've always considered the Sylvie family to be the classic All-American Family because they always seemed so close.

Prior to dinner we had the opportunity to walk outside the campsite, but the best part was when we joined up in the great room and played floor hockey. The space was enormous, with a huge fireplace and a big stuffed buck mounted above the mantle of the fireplace. The whole room had such a rustic look to it, and I had never seen anything like it. The place was a popular campsite for kids, and I was so surprised when, later in my life, my daughter Gina and I went to a campout as part of our YMCA Indian Princesses group at the very same camp. I only put two and two together when I saw the great room with that huge buck still adorning the fireplace. It all came flooding back to me.

The floor hockey was great, and my street hockey experience really came in handy. I was so happy that I was able to play well—I even scored a few goals. I was always the smallest kid in any group, but if we were involved in a sporting activity, I managed to hold my own with my quickness and coordination, and I was able to contribute despite my small stature.

Sports were an important equalizer for me, and I worked hard at trying to improve at any game that I could play. Unlike all the sports camps that were available to my kids when they were growing up, we relied on the streets and the alleys of Chicago and competing with the neighborhood kids to enjoy and develop in sports.

We had dinner together as a class, and after we talked for what seemed like forever. Finally, we fell asleep in our bunks. I slept so well that night that I didn't wake up until the morning light came in through the windows of our room. As I woke up, I felt something strange on my neck and face. After placing my hand on my neck, I cautiously brought my hand in front of my face. I saw clumps of white stuff, which upon closer inspection was shaving cream. I also knew that shaving cream was probably all over my face and hair. I looked in the bathroom mirror and confirmed it.

I got so angry. I immediately thought that Fernando, one of my classmates, was the culprit. Luckily for me, Gary and I were the only ones that were up. Gary was chuckling at my face. I told him that it wasn't that funny, but he told me to relax and that it was "no big deal."

However, it was a big deal to me, because I was convinced it was a kid that I did not always get along with who did it. I went over to Fernando's bed and woke him up.

"Hey, why did you put shaving cream on my face in the night?"

"What? It wasn't me," he answered sleepily. "I was sleeping all night."

Fernando and I were not the best of friends and it was only a few weeks prior to the campout that we had gotten into a fight. He was the second smallest boy in our 8th grade class, and felt it was his right to pick on me because I was the smallest.

One day, Fernando was with a couple of his friends, and caught up with me and my brothers while we were walking back home from school. He came up from behind and knocked my books from my hand.

I turned around and yelled at him. "Hey, what did you do that for?"

My two brothers were behind me and I could see that that they were getting nervous.

Fernando just kept laughing and told me he would do it again if he wanted to. Normally, I would never even think about getting into a fight with anyone in my class because they were all about a foot taller than me, but Fernando was a little closer to my height (even though he outweighed me).

My internal monologue told me that if I let this kid push me around this one time, he could make hell for me the rest of the year. I started yelling back at him. I'm not sure what came over me, because I rarely showed anger towards anyone in school, and even Fernando seemed a little surprised that I was pushing back.

I started getting nervous, like I usually do when I sense trouble, but that time I held my ground. He gave me a little push and then backed up as I started to fall back, but I kept my balance.

That was it. I blew my top and charged him with my fists in the air. I figured even though he was bigger than me, he wasn't all that coordinated: I would be able get in a couple of punches because I was quicker than him. I tried to land a couple of the left jabs that I had learned watching Muhammad Ali box, but all we ended up doing was rolling around locked up on the Hermitage Avenue sidewalk.

It turned out to be the only fight of my whole life, and even though it was not exactly a clear win, it gave me a little respect. My brothers also seemed to give me a look like, *Wow—I didn't know George could do that.*

Fernando didn't give me any more trouble, but I still didn't like him; which was why I was questioning why he put shaving cream on my face.

However, I don't think he wanted to have another fight with me and so told me in a convincing way that he was not the one who put shaving cream on my face.

It was then that someone yelled out that it was one of the girls who had done it. Apparently, a couple of the other boys also got shaving cream on their faces. Now that I knew I was not the only one, all the tension and anger lifted from my face, and I also started to laugh. It was then that Patricia, one of the girls from our class, came around to me and told me that she had gotten me. I was surprised that it was her, because she was usually well behaved.

"The rat always get the cheese," she said as she ran out of the room. I wasn't entirely sure what it meant, but everyone started laughing out loud, so I joined in. Many years later, I connected with Patricia on a social media page. I jokingly reminded her that she put shaving cream on my face back in 8ᵗʰ grade. She wrote back to apologize, saying that it was only for fun, but she ended the message again with, "*The rat always gets the cheese.*" For the life of me, I still couldn't figure what it meant, but it brought up memories of that great camping trip from 8ᵗʰ grade.

I found out that one of the priests at St. Boniface elementary school and church taught at a local high school in Chicago. The school was called Quigley North, but I didn't know too much more about it. None of the other older neighborhood kids I knew were attending it. Apparently, Father Stalzer, one of our three parish priests, had already spoken to my parents about Quigley at a schoolboard meeting. He thought it would be a good fit for me since I was a good student and it was "a good Catholic school."

My parents really liked the idea of me going to a high school that was highly rated academically since the local neighborhood options were not the greatest. From his experience teaching, my dad did not want to send me to a public school, and he liked the idea that Quigley was a Catholic school.

My parents really only had two concerns, but they were pretty big ones. First of all, the tuition at the high school was beyond their income level. And secondly, the school was in downtown Chicago. Father Stalzer explained to my mom and dad that he would make sure I got a partial scholarship and assistance with the tuition. He would also help me get a part-time job at the school to help with the tuition.

Father Stalzer, who advised my parents to send me to Quigley North.
He was a parish priest at St. Boniface and taught math at Quigley

Additionally, he offered to drive me to Quigley in the mornings when
he left from St. Boniface, so all I had to do was take the bus back home,
which he insisted was not that difficult. My mom was already taking the
bus downtown, so she knew the bus system, but my parents were still a
little nervous about me taking the bus downtown by myself.

Father Stalzer suggested that I sign up for "mini week" at Quigley,
which was meant for 8th graders to get a chance to experience the high
school. I told him that I didn't want to become a priest, so why would I
want to go there? He explained to me that even though it was a preparatory
seminary, only a small percentage of kids went on to become priests and
every student had the choice.

It turned out that we had four boys from my 8th grade class going to the
mini week at Quigley. Gary and Andrew and I had become good friends, so
I jumped at the idea of going to visit Quigley with the two of them. Father

Stalzer was going to drive us there and back, so we were in good hands.

I didn't realize until much later in life that after their conversation with Father Stalzer, my parents had decided to send me to Quigley. Little did I know in 8th grade that they had already spoken to Father Stalzer about sending me to Quigley, and if I came home without too many complaints, I was destined for Quigley North Preparatory Seminary High School to become a Norseman.

Mini week at Quigley was incredible. I absolutely loved the school, and it was set right in the middle of Downtown Chicago on Rush and Chestnut. This was only a block away from Michigan Avenue, which was the center of the shopping district known as "The Magnificent Mile." The old Chicago Water Tower, which was one of the few buildings to survive the fire of 1871, and the John Hancock building, my favorite, were just a few blocks away.

Quigley North (a replica of a French cathedral) was nestled among the giant skyscrapers of Chicago with Oak Street Beach and Lake Michigan nearby. What was not to like? It had everything.

As the program went on, I really liked the family atmosphere at Quigley. It was technically a seminary at that point, but it was expanding their student base by lifting many of the requirements that only admitted students who were serious about the priesthood. Most of the teachers were priests, and the ones I met that week were extremely nice.

We played basketball in their huge gym. Little did I realize that this was one of the smallest gyms a high school could have, with little space between the hoop and the back wall. If you were not careful, you could smack your head right on the walls after a layup. Luckily, they were padded in green (reminiscent of the Wrigley Field ivy where the Chicago Cubs play baseball), but it still hurt when crashing into that padding. This was the first time that I had seen an indoor basketball court, since most of the pick-up games that we had in the neighborhood were either at an outdoor hoop at a local school or the hoop in the dirt-covered backyard of my friend Jimmy.

We got a tour of the whole place and, coming from a small elementary school like St. Boniface, I was awestruck by all the facilities at Quigley. They had a library, lockers for all the students, an auditorium, a swimming pool, and a beautiful chapel with some of the most beautiful stained glass that I had ever seen. It was all overwhelming, since I had never been inside a real high school and I couldn't wait to go.

When I got home, I told my parents that this is where I want to go to high school. I noticed they both had a slight smile on their faces, knowing that that's where they were planning to send me.

Eighth grade passed by quickly, and soon spring was upon us. Mr. Cichon announced that, through Mayor Richard Daley Sr.'s program, our entire class had tickets to go see the Chicago White Sox, one of the two baseball teams in Chicago.

Most of us in class who cared for baseball were all Chicago Cubs fans, the more popular team in Chicago. I had the opportunity to go to a couple of Cub games with my dad's friend, Uncle Richard, and they were fun, but I mostly focused on the hot dogs and pop that we had at that time. Since then I had been watching and playing a lot more baseball. I couldn't hit the ball all that far, but I was becoming a good fielder. I played recreational baseball and softball well into my forties, and the tag on me was always "good glove, but can't really hit that well."

Even though it was a Sox game, because I was going with my friends, I was looking forward to spending time with them. When we got to Comiskey Park on the Southside, I found out that we had right field bleacher seats. This was my first time sitting in the outfield, and I was hoping I'd be able to catch a ball on a home run.

I don't remember who won, but I had so much fun eating peanuts and hot dogs with all my classmates that I became a Sox fan for life after that night. I was staring to figure out that the Cubs franchise was the richer of the two, with a full house every day and a big TV contract. In comparison, the Sox couldn't fill their stadium and usually ended up close to last place year after year in the early seventies. I always liked rooting for the underdog, and the Sox were a good fit.

Soon after the Sox game, we were in full preparation mode for graduation, and I was getting a little nervous about high school. On the last day of school, everyone was busy signing each other's autograph book. This tradition did not survive: when I told my kids about it, they said I was a nerd. But everyone in my class had it. St. Boniface was not big enough to have a yearbook, so this was the next best thing.

There was a lot of creative, colorful writing that went into the final statements that classmates made to each other, but I will always treasure it. I still have my 8th grade autograph book, and I still get a chuckle as I read through the various entries.

We had some colorful characters in the 8th grade class. There were only twenty kids in total, with eight boys and twelve girls. Graduation day came and went, and I became a teenager, done with elementary school and ready to go to high school.

As I walked around with my neighborhood friends, I felt grown up, since I was the oldest of the bunch and the only one going to high school. During the ceremony I did choke up because St. Boniface had provided a lot of great memories, and I'd met some great people that helped me adjust to the American way of life. As I reflected back, I thought about of how difficult it had been on that first day in 5th grade, when I felt everyone was always staring at me and grinning; by the time I left St. Boniface, I was just one of the kids, ready to go to high school. I was on top of the world.

I had many friends at school, and there really was not anyone that I didn't get along with. Even Fernando, the kid I'd had the fight with, became a friend. The kids at school came from all different backgrounds and ethnicities, and I felt comfortable adjusting to each individual personally. The school has long since been torn down, but whenever I drive by that church steeple staring at me on the highway, I always go back to my elementary school days and have only great memories.

Summer came and went quickly that year in Chicago. The city came alive during the summer. Families in the neighborhoods could be seen outside all the time. You could see people sitting on the front stoops of the houses lining Augusta Boulevard in my neighborhood. My friend Jimmy's house was on that street. It was a traditional two story house with a small basement, which was typical in Chicago.

Sometimes in the summer, when it was too hot to play outside or raining, we would play indoor hockey in Jimmy's basement. The entrance was in the back of the house with flat, bunker-style doors. The basement was primarily used for storage, and contained the water heater and furnace. Somehow, we managed to clear some space so that we could play hockey with our sticks in that cramped space. How six preteen kids could play hockey down there I'll never know, but in between all the boxes, the dryer and washing machine we were able to shoot pucks at a goalie.

Summer was always exciting, since we could play in the street, the alley, or Jimmy's backyard for hours on end. Jimmy's mom would sometime make us steak tacos, which were some of the best I've ever tasted. They consisted of what looked to be just a tortilla and a piece of meat, but they tasted so good after playing. The days were carefree, and all we did was play all day long.

Little did I know how my life was going to change as I headed into high school. I still met and played with my neighborhood friends while in high school, but not as often. We were starting to outgrow the alley and the small dirt yard behind Jimmy's house, and that feeling of sheer pleasure when meeting up with my friends near the alley never felt the same after that summer.

PART III: CHICAGO FOREVER

CHAPTER 15

HOGWARTS IN CHICAGO

Quigley North in downtown Chicago

The year was 2009. We were all in downtown Chicago, right on the Magnificent Mile. My wife, Suma, and my kids, Gina and Matthew, were with me. We had just come from the Nike store on Michigan Avenue, which my son had been begging us forever to take him to.

I was about to hail a taxi to head to the train station, but I turned back around and spoke to Gina and Matthew. "Hey, would you guys like to see where Dad went to high school?"

"Do we have to Dad? I want to get home and try on my new shoes," Matthew replied as he looked at his new pair of shoes in the Nike bag for the tenth time.

"I want to go see it Dad!" Gina said excitedly. "Is this the place that looks like Hogwarts in Harry Potter?" She had previously seen pictures of my high school. She had also read all the Harry Potter books many times over during her teenage years and could recite many of the chapters by heart. She and her friends would routinely act out the scenes in our back patio on endless hot summer days.

The Hogwarts comparison was a little bit of a stretch, but Quigley had that look. One day I had mentioned to Gary Sylvie, my first American friend, that Gina had said that Quigley North High School looked like Hogwarts, and he replied that his daughter had mentioned the very same comparison.

Suma and Gina finally convinced Matthew that it would be fun to see Dad's old school, so we headed north on Michigan Avenue towards the John Hancock building. We made a left on Chestnut Street and made our way to the side entrance of Quigley North High School. Looking up from the sidewalk, I marveled at the gothic building with gabled roofs and spires that reached out to the sky, although it was dwarfed by the surrounding downtown skyscrapers. After our arrival, I spread my arms out wide and proudly told everyone, "Here it is."

Quigley North, built in 1917, is located in downtown Chicago on Chestnut and Rush, two blocks west of Michigan Avenue. In 1916, Cardinal George Mundelein announced plans for the building of a preparatory seminary in the early French Gothic style of architecture in downtown Chicago. He named the school in honor of his predecessor, Archbishop James Edward Quigley. Echoing the educational theories of Johan Wolfgang Goethe (a German literary writer and statesman), Cardinal Mundelein surrounded Quigley students with great architectural beauty. It is one of the most beautiful buildings in Chicago and, nestled among the modern skyscrapers surrounding it, instills a stark yet very appealing contrast to its neighborhood.

Quigley's St. James chapel, with stained glass modeled after Sainte-Chapelle in Paris, was designed by architect Taylor Davis. It has been listed on the National Register of Historic places since 1996. The Quigley North seminaries have educated a number of priests, cardinals, and bishops.

Suma had seen Quigley before on a previous visit a few years after we got married, so she was familiar with the building. Both Gina and Matthew had quizzical looks on their faces as we stood next to the gothic-looking building. This school certainly did not look like any of the schools back in the suburbs where we resided.

I knew that Quigley had been closed down for a few years, but I was still hoping to get in and show my children my old stomping grounds. I stepped up to the door to get in, but the door was locked. After peeking through the window on the side of the door for about five minutes, I finally caught the attention of someone walking inside.

He opened the door and immediately said, "Sorry folks: the school is shut down, and it does not allow any visitors."

I saw the look of disappointment in Gina's face so I quickly told the gentleman, who looked like a handyman, some sentimental details to convince him to let us in and take a look around. I told him I was a Quigley North Norseman thirty years ago, and I just wanted to walk around for a few minutes so that I can show my kids where I went to high school.

He looked at us with a quizzical look darting between me and my family for a good ten seconds and then finally acquiesced. "Ah, alright! Thirty years ago, wow; I guess I can let you in for a little while."

I thanked him. "Don't worry, I still remember where everything is so we'll be quick."

"You can take a little time to look around," he said amicably, "but just close the door on the way out." With that, he was on his way down the hall to get back to whatever he had been doing.

I climbed up the small set of stairs to get to the main floor with my family. I caught sight of the main hall and the front office, which had wall-to-ceiling wood paneling. I stopped in my tracks and stared blankly ahead as all the memories of my first day at Quigley in the fall of '73 came flooding back.

CHAPTER 16

"HERE WE GO NORSEMEN, HERE WE GO"

Class in session

"Hey, what's your problem?" I yelled out as I was pushed from behind. "Shut up, Freshie, before I beat the shit out of you," the tough-looking kid shouted back. He was about six feet tall and possessed more facial hair than he really should for a high schooler.

I turned around to face him where he stood, towering over me. He took a swipe at my waist. I really thought he was going to hit me, but he only caught my right hand cradled around my stack of books. My books flew out of my hands as I climbed the stairs to get to my homeroom on my first day of high school.

He quickly turned away and went on to antagonize the next freshman in line. I was about to yell out something, but since I was not really hurt, I decided that it was probably not a good idea to continue the conversation with the sophomore goon. Instead, I tried to recover all my books.

Luckily the stairs were packed with other kids, and I didn't fall back down and break my neck. As I was getting knocked around by other kids, I tried to retrieve all my books. I noticed I was not the only one in this predicament, as other freshmen were also getting bowled over by sophomores who shared our wing of the building on the second floor.

I'm not sure who in school administration thought it was a good idea to put freshmen and sophomores in the same wing. Freshmen lockers were on the first floor of the west wing, and the sophomores had their lockers on the second floor. And as tradition goes for the first week at Quigley of a new school year, the sophomores wreaked havoc on the freshmen while the faculty turned a blind eye so long as no one was in danger of immediate death. Funny, they did not tell us about any of this during orientation or the mini week that took place in 8th grade when I had first visited Quigley.

I finally collected all my books and made my way up the stairs to find where my homeroom was. I had no idea what actually happened in a homeroom. Unfortunately, I had forgotten to ask some of the high school kids that I knew over the summer, and my mom had no idea what it was, either. I wish I would've covered these issues with my dad the previous evening when he asked me if I had any burning questions before I started high school. I had said no, and that I was good with everything. My mom told me that she was sure that if I had any questions or concerns that one of the second-year students would help me if I asked them. Ha! If she only knew what I was going through on my first day, she would probably have pulled me out of that school immediately. My parents thought it would be a very safe environment for me because it was a seminary, but that first week felt more like something out of the book *Lord of the Flies.*

I was late for homeroom, but so were many other kids, so I didn't feel too bad. The homeroom teacher (who was also going to be my math teacher), Mrs. Rellehan, was actually very nice and welcomed us into the class. I think she had a pretty good idea of the morning we all had. Mrs. Rellehan was one of the few lay teachers at Quigley; ninety-five percent of the faculty were priests. She was young and beautiful with long, blonde hair. Many of the kids had these silly grins on their faces.

When we all settled into our seats, we all found out very quickly that Mrs. Rellehan was also a very strong lady who was not going to be pushed around. She quickly took control of her class. All the silly grins and conversations about her looks stopped in an instant.

Unfortunately, none of the kids from my elementary school at St. Boniface were in my homeroom, so I was on my own to navigate the morning classes. I managed to avoid the sophomores during the transition of classes until at last lunchtime came around. After wasting valuable time trying to figure out exactly where the cafeteria was, I luckily found my friend Gary walking through an entrance to get to the lunch line. I made my way up to where he was in line and felt a lot better when I saw a friendly, familiar face.

We went to sit down at an open table but were quickly told to leave because apparently it was a sophomore table. We started looking around for the freshman tables, which were of course unmarked, but finally saw some kids with the same confused looks we had and sat down near them. As we ate our sloppy joes and tater tots, Gary and I exchanged our run-ins with the sophomores from the morning. He mentioned that if I used the staircase at the opposite end of the hallway I would be able to avoid them.

In the afternoon I had a free period, so I checked out the library. I knew that Father Stalzer from St. Boniface (the priest that had recommended Quigley to me) had made arrangements with the school so that I would work after school starting the second week, and the money I earned from it would go against my tuition. I wanted to see where I needed to go after classes were over. I needed to stay about thirty minutes three times a week to vacuum the floors and clean the desks, after which I could go home.

As I walked in, it didn't sound like a normal library. I expected a very quiet place, but there were kids yelling and paper airplanes being thrown everywhere. A quick look at the drop-tile ceiling showed an array of ballpoint pens and pencils randomly decorated it. I also shockingly noticed that a cigarette was placed in the raised hand of St. Joseph's statue near the entrance of the library. The librarian priest, who had a small office with a glass front in the back of the library, kept coming out to get the kids to quiet down, but no one paid attention. He would go back into his office and then would come out again a few minutes later with his index finger on his pursed lips.

It was very strange seeing him coming in and out of his office. Every time he came out the kids got rowdier: they kept calling out like a herd of goats in unison, "Maaaa, Maaaa." This was apparently his nickname. The librarian priest had been at Quigley for a number of years, but he was not all that firm, so some kids took advantage of him. He was part of the old guard, who thought everyone should be good seminarians and if you were not going to seriously pursue the priesthood, you shouldn't be there. I couldn't believe that they put someone so unable to keep control over a group of kids in charge of the library, where kids were free to do anything they wanted.

After looking around a little, I walked to an open table to do some reading, where I almost ran into a giant of a man walking into the library. This guy was the tallest guy I had ever come across, and as we passed each other I had a good look at his belt buckle. I later found out that he was one of the teachers at Quigley and one of the basketball coaches.

It turns out that the other teachers would take turns to sit at the library reception area, and he was the person that actually watched over the kids. Unfortunately, the transition time between classes left the librarian priest exposed for a brief time, during which the kids ran amok. The library got real quiet as Mr. Ansett, the basketball coach and Spanish teacher, took up his perch at the reception desk. I took a quick glance at the back office, where the librarian priest had a look of relief on his face. He went back to his desk to do whatever he did back there.

Such was the set up at the library. Luckily for me there weren't too many troublemakers there after classes ended for the day, so I was able to get my work done quickly and then head home.

Later that first week I met my "Big Brother" at Quigley, Ed. Ed was a senior at Quigley and was assigned to me as my Big Brother. He was the one that I would be able to go to if I had any issues, and was supposed to watch over me. I was not sure how it was going to work and really had very little expectations that my Big Brother would be of any help. But one day this huge, blond-haired senior came over and introduced himself as my Big Brother. He was such an extremely friendly face and was genuinely interested in helping me adjust to Quigley. He assured me that I could come to him for anything that I wanted to know about the workings of Quigley.

I would see Ed once in a while, and he always made time to come over and say hello and ask if everything was going well. The first few months at Quigley were somewhat hectic and confusing for me, and it was always refreshing to see Ed's friendly face. I only met with him just a few more times that first year, but it was very cool to have a senior and varsity basketball player say hello to me in front of my freshman classmates.

The way Ed treated me that first week of my freshman year was the definition of a Big Brother, and I was grateful that he was assigned to me. I also found out that Ed was a star athlete in basketball and an honor roll student. He definitely embodied the Quigley North Norsemen spirit. I thought back on how Ed treated me that freshman year at Quigley many times as I came across similar situations with other people who were new to a country, a job, or generally just someone who needed a friend to talk to. I never forgot Ed, and I was positive he wouldn't remember me when, much later in life, I sent him an invite on social media. To my surprise, he did remember me and accepted my invitation.

CHAPTER 17

ELEVATOR KEYS AND CHAPEL SLIPPERS

Playing Risk in Mr McGreals's history class

Things started settling down after a few weeks when the sophomores got tired of hazing us every morning. I began to figure out where I needed to go, and quickly got the lay of the land. The Quigley structure was arranged in a concentric, rectangular shape, with two floors and an open courtyard that housed the parking lot in the center with a majestic, arched entrance for vehicles to park inside. The freshman lockers on the first floor and the sophomores on the second occupied the west side of the building, and directly across the courtyard, on the east side, were the juniors and seniors. The gym and library were on the north end, and the cafeteria sat parallel with the chapel on the south end. The chapel also had its own entrance from Rush Street on the west side.

Every morning, when Father Stalzer pulled into the arched entrance of the courtyard with us to park his car, it was easy to notice the green, oxidized gabled spires on the chapel and the main building that reached into the downtown sky. However, it was still dwarfed by all of the skyscrapers surrounding the gothic structure.

I started seeing familiar faces in my classes and the cafeteria, and I quickly started making some friends. I was the only Asian kid in Quigley, but after a few months I felt like I belonged there with all my classmates. In addition to the boys from my grade school I met Tim, Chris, and Larry, who had an uncanny resemblance to a young Harry Potter with his round glasses.

I was sitting in the cafeteria with my new friends Larry and Chris one afternoon, eating our cheeseburgers and fries, when this kid named Gerhardt, who looked like a giant to me at the time, sat with us. He was giving advice to his buddy Larry about stuff that the sophomores were trying to sell us.

"Don't get fooled into buying any of the elevator passes or chapel slippers," cautioned Gerhardt. "It's an ongoing gag that sophomores try to goad freshman into buying."

There was only one elevator in the building, and all students were prohibited from using it. It was strictly for faculty. The sophomore students, however, would try to convince the freshmen that with the special passes, one would be able to use the elevators, making it easier to get to classes on time. There were also rumors going around that sophomores were selling chapel slippers that they claimed were mandatory to wear when we went into the chapel for mass or a memorial service, which happened at least once a week. Despite the details, I never actually saw an elevator pass or chapel slipper, and I never knew of anyone who was duped by the sophomores.

Quigley North was located on Rush Street, right in the middle of downtown, close to the night club scene and adult entertainment establishments that populated the area back then mere blocks away. Many of the sophomores kept trying to remind the incoming freshmen about the Candy Hut, where "they sold the best candy in the city," but most of us knew that it was actually a strip bar. I never made it to the Candy Hut, but there were a couple of freshmen that I heard went to take a look and got a big surprise when they found that the Candy Hut was not really a candy store. Again, I quickly surmised these were more likely stories than actual events, but it sure sounded great, and all of us repeated it to our friends; it made for great conversation.

At Quigley, it was important to get to class on time, because if you were late you were given a demerit. This was a Catholic high school, and a seminary at that, so there were lots of rules. We all had to wear blue or black pants with a dress shirt and tie. We had to wear dress shoes, which I absolutely dreaded. Gym shoes were strictly prohibited, and if you wore them you ended up with a demerit. A demerit was also handed out if you forgot your gym shoes for gym class. You couldn't win.

If you didn't abide by the dress code or not follow any of the numerous rules, you were assigned demerits. At the beginning of every quarter every student was assigned a demerit card with twenty-five spaces printed on one side of the card. You were also given a list of rules that needed to be followed and the demerits that would be given out if you broke the rule. Each time one of the teachers caught you breaking a rule, they could assign you anywhere from one to ten demerits.

You could get one or two demerits for being late, not being in uniform, not having your athletic supporter for gym class, or talking back to the teacher. Higher offenses like smoking in the bathroom, getting into a fight, or cursing at the teacher would get you five on the spot. You could also get an additional five demerits to what was already recorded if you lost your demerit card. For every five demerits you racked up, you had to serve "Jug" (more on that later), and if you were unfortunate enough to collect twenty-five demerits in one quarter, or sixty demerits in one school calendar year, you were expelled.

You were also assigned a behavior grade on your report card, so you could not hide the number of demerits you received from your parents. I think knowing that my parents would see an actual grade on the report card was what stressed me out the most. I was a pretty well-behaved kid for the most part, but you could rack up demerits for just being forgetful.

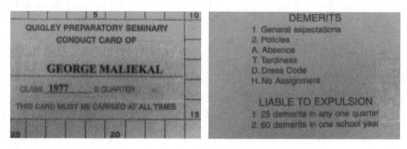

Demerit Card front (left), Demerit Card rear (right)

The disciplinary operations at Quigley when I attended were supervised by one of the priests, named Father Thaddeus Jakubowski. All of us addressed him as Father Jakubowski, but when speaking with each other, the students referred to him as "Big Jake," or sometimes just "Jake" after you got to know him a little. I always referred to him as Big Jake when talking to other students, and only when I became an adult did I actually start referring to him as Jake when speaking with classmates. He also taught classes at Quigley, but I always viewed him as the sheriff of Quigley North, and a scary one at that. He was a tall and imposing figure, especially when walking the halls, with long sideburns and a scowl he wore during my freshman year.

I tried not to make eye contact when I saw Big Jake because I didn't want him questioning me. Others had mentioned to me that once you got to know him, he was not a bad guy, but I never got to know him and he always scared the hell out of me, especially that first year.

Anytime you walked down the halls at Quigley there was dead silence when Big Jake was spotted. I'm not sure I ever saw him smile and I always felt that he was going to draw his pen from his side shirt pocket and assign me demerits just because he felt like it.

This was the way I saw him as a thirteen-year-old freshman at Quigley, but later as an adult I learned that Father Jakubowski had a very long and distinguished career as a priest and was named auxiliary Bishop of Chicago in 1988. He continued to serve his community in meaningful ways after retirement until he passed away in 2013.

Father Jakubowski, QN disciplanarian.
His scowl that I remembered as a freshman looks more like a smile now

Big Jake also chaired many of the "Jug" sessions. As I previously mentioned, for every five demerits you received, you had to serve Jug. During Jug you had to sit in a classroom after school with other students serving Jug, where you had to write out the classic poem "The Raven" by Edgar Allan Poe in cursive, using your best penmanship, for an hour with Big Jake staring down at you. I only served Jug one time in my years at Quigley, and it came in that freshman year, mainly because I was late for class or I forgot to wear all of my uniform to gym class (usually my athletic supporter, which I absolutely hated wearing. It was the goofiest thing I had ever seen, and I'm not sure exactly what it did).

Mr. Schaefer, our PE teacher, who was a good guy but was somewhat of a tyrant when it came to the full uniform in PE class, was always giving out demerits if you didn't show up dressed appropriately. My parents were shocked to see that I got a "B" that first quarter because my five demerits in one quarter dropped my grade down from an "A."

I'm not sure the strict level of discipline that was at Quigley actually worked on everyone. Many of the students rebelled even harder as the demerits piled up. They must have figured they were going to get kicked out soon, so they were even wilder. There were a number of kids kicked out of school by the end of my freshman year because they had accumulated twenty-five demerits or more in one quarter. Even though Quigley was a seminary, some of the kids managed to get five to ten demerits at a time. I saw one kid get ten demerits because the teacher caught him leaning out from a second-floor window throwing metal-tipped darts at a car parked on the street that had a vinyl roof, which was popular in the mid-seventies. Vinyl roofs on cars went out of style pretty quickly, probably because people were likely throwing all kinds of things at it to see if it would stick on or rip the vinyl.

A few months into my freshman year, things were going relatively smoothly. I was doing well in my classes and made a number of new friends. The freshman class that year had its share of troublemakers, and a handful of students were expelled after the first semester. We had started out as a class of about eighty-five, and after the first semester it was already down to eighty.

A couple of the students were expelled because they set fire to the auditorium curtains on the main stage. Luckily the fire was contained immediately, and no one was hurt. I had a hard time figuring out how some of these kids could be so ignorant of their actions.

The expulsions didn't stop at five, because there were still several students who were pushing the envelope of the Quigley North disciplinary procedures. I always wondered how a school like Quigley allowed kids that were real troublemakers, and only later in life did I learn that during my time there, they were relaxing their academic standards so that enrollment would increase, ultimately leading to more priests being ordained.

I was really afraid of one of the boys in my freshman class. Let's call him Darryl. Darryl was a tall, caramel-skinned kid with a short, matching caramel afro. He seemed to walk with a glide when he approached you and spoke in reassuring tones. Darryl liked to show off his neck hold technique, which would render the victim unconscious for a short period. After his victim came to, he would laugh eerily and move on to his next victim.

I'm not sure exactly where he picked up this nasty little trick, but he would always try to get any kid that was smaller than him in this neck hold. I'm really unclear what the motivation was for him to do this to his classmates, but I tried to avoid him at all cost. My two-prong strategy with Darryl was to avoid him as much as possible and only to be in his presence when some of my bigger friends were with me. My radar was always up when I roamed the halls as a freshman, and whenever I saw him from a distance, especially in an empty hallway, I usually doubled back and found a new route to where I needed to go. I managed to avoid him my entire freshman year, and, fortunately for me (and the rest of us, if I'm being honest), he was kicked out in his second year.

I was the second-shortest kid out of the whole freshman class, narrowly beating out the shortest kid by about a quarter of an inch. It bothered me initially. On top of being undersized for my age in both height and weight, I was a full year younger than the other entire freshman class because of the transition I made from the Indian school system and having an early birthdate.

Being the only Asian student at Quigley and the second-shortest kid in the freshman class was not a good combination. I got my share of ribbing, mostly because of my height and small stature. I don't ever remember anyone poking fun at me directly because I was the only Asian kid at school, and never ran across any situation where kids were teasing me or bullying me because I was Indian.

Sometimes, just like the snakes in the shallow waters of the rice fields I thought I saw back in Kerala, I felt like all eyes were on me whenever I walked into a room full of kids that I did not know, especially that first year at Quigley. I quickly reminded myself that I was letting my imagination get the best of me and learned to move on towards the end of the year.

Even my dad got into the act of calling out my small size one time when I was showing off my muscles at home. He called me the "Cornish hen." He was just joking, but I did not like it at all. I was extremely sensitive about my size, and no matter how much I ate I could not gain any weight or height.

One of my most embarrassing moments in high school was the time I was forced into a locker. I was hanging around with a few of my friends near our lockers, getting ready for class, when a couple of the troublemakers came at us and gave us a hard time. I tried not to escalate the situation by over-reacting, hoping they would go away, but they were going to have some fun and *I* was going to be their fun that day. My friends started backing up since they didn't want to be the next victim.

Two kids I didn't know well grabbed hold of me and pushed me into an empty locker and shut the door. They kept pushing at the door and closed the latch so that I couldn't get out. I was happy that it was just an unused locker, so there was no combination lock on it. I could hear my friends trying to reopen the door, but they were held back by the bigger kids. I was getting a little frantic, pushing at the door, but it would not open.

This went on for about a minute, but then it became very quiet. One of the teachers was seen approaching down the hall so they quickly abandoned their bullying and ran off. I burst out of the locker and fell to the floor because the door latch was now released. My friends asked me if I was okay. I tried to brush it off as no big deal, even though I was thoroughly embarrassed that I got locked into a locker in front of my friends.

As usual, I kept the incident to myself and didn't tell the teacher who walked by shortly after I got out. I also did not mention it to my parents, and thankfully my friends that were witness to the incident never brought it up again.

I did see one of the kids who had shoved me in the locker later that afternoon, and he came by and attempted an apology. "Hey man, I was just goofing around. I also appreciate that you didn't say anything to the teacher."

I looked at this guy, dumbfounded. "I could still tell someone you know," I said before walking away. He had a nervous look on his face when I said this, and he took a step towards me, but he stopped. I just kept walking, not turning back.

I told myself that day that something like that would never happen to me again. I knew I needed to be a little more vocal and speak my mind the next time I was being pushed around.

After I had settled down the next day, I realized that it really was no big deal and that they were just having some fun, but it stung deeply, and it was one of those moments that I never forgot. As embarrassing as it was, it was also an important turning point for me realizing that I had to stand up for myself. I told the story of being locked in a locker to my kids one time, and they started howling with laughter.

The locker incident was a low point in my freshman year that will always stick with me, but I also had some high points. Up until that year, I never cared too much about what happened in the world, especially history. Mr. McGreal changed all that.

Mr. McGreal was one of the teachers I had who was *not* a priest.

Freshman history class was exceptional. Mr. McGreal was a motivating figure, not only because of what he knew, but because of the way in which he taught. He brought history to life.

Mr. McGreal, QN History Teacher—He was my favorite

I still remember to this day how we started of our first lesson about World War II. He laid out six games of the board game Risk and told us to form groups of six around the board.

"The best way to learn about World War II is to actually participate," he told us.

The game of Risk pitted the Allied powers against the Axis powers, and even though it was just a board game that looked to control countries with a roll of the dice, it set a perfect backdrop for what we were about to study.

Mr. McGreal had a style about him that I found inspiring. He was knowledgeable about his subject matter, composed, and made it fun for students to learn. Fast forwarding to the present and in my career, I would always try to emulate the composure I saw in Mr. McGreal.

Another one of my favorite teachers at Quigley was Father Cahill. When I first attended my freshman year English class, I was surprised to see a priest that was as big as he was: he looked like he could tear you apart. He was built like a marine. He looked much older to me, because he had short white hair, but he always wore a short-sleeved black shirt with a priest's collar that exposed his powerful forearms.

Father Cahill seemed tough when you initially met him, but he was actually a gentle soul. He taught us English in a straightforward way. He was tough and made you work in his class. His signature moment was his daily quizzes that had to be taken on a yellow unlined pad of paper, which you could get at the book store. This was a big portion of the final grade you received, so you had to be prepared. He made it clear that if you did not have the yellow pad, you were not allowed to take the quiz and would get a failing grade for that quiz.

Father Cahill unfortunately passed away later in my senior year. During a conversation with Mr. McGreal recently, Father Cahill's name was brought up, and he told me he always remembers Father Cahill looking up at him in the faculty lounge with a "cheroot in one hand and a twinkle in his eye." I had to look up to see what a "cheroot" was and found out that it was a cigar with both the ends cut. I never saw Father Cahill smoke a cigar, but I could definitely see that look on him.

CHAPTER 18

COP CONFRONTATION

Chicago style Polish sausage

One day during my freshman year, I convinced my mom that I was sick and should be allowed to stay home. I did have a slight cold, and maybe a slight fever, but I played it up and convinced my parents that I should stay home and rest. Classes at Quigley were only getting tougher, and I figured I needed some time off. Both my parents were working and my brothers were in school, so I'd have the house all to myself. I figured I'd watch TV all day and maybe go and grab a "Polish" during lunch at my favorite hot dog stand near our house, on the other side of the street.

As everyone started shuffling out of the house, I was still in bed trying to cough a little louder so everyone would know that I was sick.

My mom came by before she left to check in on me. "Now, don't watch TV all day, and make sure that you get enough rest so that you'll be well enough to go to school tomorrow. I don't want to you to miss another day."

"Don't worry Mom, I'll probably just sleep most of the day."

The morning went relatively smoothly as I tried to watch as much TV as possible. After watching *Bewitched*, *I Dream of Genie*, *Green Acres*, and the *Beverly Hillbillies*, I got a little bored. I had a second bowl of cereal, Count Chocula (my favorite), but I was still hungry. My mom had made me baloney sandwiches for lunch, but they just didn't appeal to me. I knew I had a couple of dollars on me, so I decided to go out and get a Chicago-style Polish sausage and fries from across the street.

This was my absolute favorite meal back then. I could get it at the local hot dog place situated right across the street from my house. I really didn't want to spend my own money on food when I was home, but my mouth was watering thinking about the Chicago-style Polish with thick-cut fries. Jumbo sausage, which was slightly bigger than a hot dog, had its own unique flavor with mustard, ketchup, tomatoes, relish, and the cherry on the top of this local classic: a layer of hot, green sport peppers, just the way I liked it.

When I was fourteen years old there wasn't any better food in the whole world. I always got a lot of flak about putting ketchup on my Polish, but this was not a hot dog. Ketchup on a Chicago-style hot dog would be blasphemy, but on a Polish was different. I just liked the way the combination of mustard and ketchup enhanced the flavor of the Polish.

It was early spring and there was still a chill in the air, so I grabbed my jacket and put on my K-Mart Pro-Keds gym shoes and went out into the world.

I arrived at the hot dog stand at about 11:30, and there was no one there because it was still early. The owner of the hot dog stand knew who I was because I'd been there several times, but I didn't know his name. He was always friendly to me, but we didn't do much more than greet each other before he took my order. I had my usual Polish, washed it down with a bottle of RC Cola (Royal Crown Cola—a Chicago favorite) and was ready to go back home. The owner gave me a quick wave to see me off.

After I crossed the street to get back to my house, I saw the typical blue lights of a Chicago cop car flashing. They were approaching quickly. After the cop car came to a stop near me, I saw him roll down the window. He shouted out to me, "Hey kid, I need you to come over here."

I was nearly home, and shocked to be confronted like this. "Who me?" I asked, pointing my thumb at my chest.

"Yeah, get in the back seat. I want to talk to you," said the cop.

I couldn't figure out for the life of me why he would want to talk to me, unless he was arresting me for jaywalking on a residential street. I opened the back door, which he unlocked, and there I was: sitting in the back seat of a Chicago police car for the first time in my life.

He didn't say anything for what seemed like fifteen minutes, but it was probably just a couple of minutes. I was getting a little scared and thought to myself, *Why did I decide not to go to school today?* Attending class at Quigley and talking with all my friends didn't seem so bad right about now.

Finally, the cop turned around from the driver's seat and interrogated me. "What are you doing on the streets in the middle of the day?"

I didn't really understand why he was asking, but I decided that even though I was scared I had to set this guy straight. I answered back with a little more strength in my voice. "I live right there," I explained, pointing to my house, "and I just went across the street to get lunch."

At this time, I noticed that the cop had a small notebook in his hand, and he was writing down everything that I said. I also got a good look at this cop: he was an older guy, with pock marks on his round face and a big head. He didn't really look all that mean.

"How do I know that's where you were? And how come you are not at school today?"

"I just told you: I was just there," I said, pointing at the hot dog place. "I felt a little sick today, so I didn't go to school."

He gave me a close look, and with a smirk said, "You don't look sick to me."

I was not sure what this guy was after, and I figured the best way to get out of this was to explain myself and be clear and specific about what I was doing. I knew I had the advantage because I hadn't done anything, and so all I had to tell him was the truth. Luckily for me, my English was getting good; I had completely lost my Indian accent, and I was getting good at explaining things to people so that they fully understood.

I moved closer to the edge of the seat, and with a little more vigor in my voice, I told him that I was staying home from my school, but I was all alone at the house. I felt a little better at lunchtime, so I thought I would go across the street and get something to eat for lunch because my parents were working and my little brothers were at school. Showing him my house key, I told him I would be happy to show him where I lived, and pointed to our apartment.

He took all this down carefully in his notebook, but he still was not giving me any clues about why I was stopped in the first place.

After thinking it through, I came out and asked him the reason as to why he even stopped me in the first place.

"Well, we just had a robbery in the area, and the word is that a couple of kids with dark complexions were seen running from the crime scene."

Then it hit me. This guy had stopped me just because I had a dark complexion. Never mind that I was all of 5" 2" inches tall, and even though I had just turned fourteen I probably looked about ten years old. I started getting a little nervous again, because I had heard stories about cops giving Latino and black kids in the neighborhood a hard time and arresting them for no reason at all. I shook that thought out of my head because this cop looked like a reasonable guy, and I felt that I would be able to clear myself pretty quickly.

"Hey, why don't you just talk to the owner of the hot dog stand back there? I just finished eating there, and I'm sure the owner would know who I am because I've eaten there a number of times."

He turned back around and started driving off with me in the back seat. Now I was getting really nervous, but I saw that he was turning back at the next block.

"Okay, let's go see him," he said, although not soon enough to keep me from freaking out a little more.

As we walked to the hot dog stand, the owner in his white T-shirt, boat shaped paper hat, and ketchup-and-mustard-stained apron came up to the counter and immediately addressed the officer. "What's going on?"

"Do you know this kid?"

"Yeah, I know him; he was just in here eating his lunch."

"Does he live around here?"

"Yeah, he lives across the street. What do you need with him?"

"Well, there have been a couple robberies in the area, and witnesses are saying it was conducted by a couple of teenagers with dark complexions."

At hearing why the cop stopped me, the owner's mouth curled to one side, his eyes squinted, and he got in the cop's face, now shouting, "What the hell are you doing? Does this kid look like a burglar to you? This is probably the nicest kid in this neighborhood, and you probably scared the hell out of him."

The cop told him to settle down, but the vendor was still furious; he continued to yell at the officer. Finally, the cop just walked out of the hot dog stand without even looking at me and just drove away.

"Stupid coppers," said the hot dog vendor. "Sometimes they don't think. Go home, kid."

I thanked him, gave him a smile, and waved goodbye before running back across the street and into the house. He went the extra mile to stick up for me when he didn't really need to; he cared about the kids in his neighborhood, no matter what their skin color was.

That left an indelible mark on me, and even though I don't remember his name, I will always remember the hot dog stand guy with the white apron and hat who went to bat for me in a sticky situation. He was a real Chicagoan. I've met many hard-working people like the hot dog stand guy who were just as compassionate and ready to step in to help if they thought a wrong was being done. I learned a lot from him that day, and when I came across similar situations that everyday individuals face, I try to step in when I can.

I don't remember ever telling anyone about the incident when I was younger, including my parents. I didn't want them to worry about me, and I learned a valuable lesson about how to communicate clearly in a difficult situation. It was empowering to me that with logic and clarity I could go a long way to diffuse a situation by using my voice and tone. I realized then that it can be as powerful as threats and intimidation, with even better outcomes. Besides, I couldn't intimidate or threaten anyone physically anyway, so I worked on my voice to control situations from getting out of hand.

As I write this incident down, I think about if it had happened in today's times. I think I would've been a little tenser just because of all the news stories that we hear on a daily basis. Thinking back on this, the cop was an okay guy who was checking out all his leads. It was irritating that my skin color still came to the top of his mind when thinking about who the burglar would be. Our inherent prejudices will always seep through, but at least he was competent enough to hear what I had to say and followed up on my story.

Confrontations like this with Chicago-area cops happened to me a few more times and, although it was extremely frustrating, I managed to have polite, respectful conversations with the police officers and managed to stay out of trouble.

The summer after my freshman year was hot and humid. There was a public swimming pool by our house, about two blocks south on Wood Street. Oddly enough, it was located right next to a police station, but you wouldn't know it by all the shady characters that usually hung out by the pool. It was the only pool nearby that I could remember, so everyone showed up on hot summer days. My mom did not like us going there, but I would take my two little brothers after my parents came home from work to cool off. It was either let us go to the pool or let the three of us make a big mess cooped up inside the house, so she usually consented.

The pool's deepest part was only three feet, and it was surrounded by a small walkway and a six-foot-high chain-link fence. Even though no one was supposed to dive into the pool, everyone did it. There were even some stupid older kids that would climb the fence and dive in the three-foot water. How they kept from splatting their head on the bottom of the pool, I'll never know.

When our friends came with us to the pool it was always fun, even though most days it was so crowded there was never any swimming going on. You just splashed around and ducked your head underwater to see how long you could hold your breath. I never won that game. Even though it was crowded, it was a great way to cool off.

That was the summer I also managed to land my first paying job. Even though I had just turned fourteen, I was part of Mayor Richard Daley Sr.'s youth program, where the city of Chicago subsidized the jobs of teenagers younger than sixteen so that we would stay off the streets and out of trouble.

There were five of us who were scheduled to paint the basement of our church, St. Boniface. I had never painted before, so I was excited, and I was going to get paid—a whole $1.10 per hour—and I was so thrilled because I'd never had that kind of money come my way. I already thought about how I was going to spend my money on albums, fast food, and as many hockey cards as I could afford.

Unfortunately, I did not get to keep any of the money I earned because, as my parents informed me, it was the Indian custom to contribute the children's earnings to the family bank account. I knew it would help my parents out, however little, so I was not too upset.

Even though I didn't get to keep any of the money, it was a great job. Danny, my classmate Gary's brother, also worked with me that summer. I did not know Danny that well, but by the end of the summer I really liked hanging out with him. We worked four days a week for five hours a day, and they fed us lunch. We would listen to the radio while we were painting, and nobody really seemed to keep a close eye on us. Danny turned me on to some great rock music beyond what I would hear on AM car radio, which set the stage for my lifelong passion for rock music.

The individuals in charge would tell us what to do at the start of the day and then pretty much leave until lunchtime when they brought us our food. We would only see them again when it was time to call it quits. I would go home with a lot of paint on me.

"George," Mom would say, "were you painting the church or each other?"

The end of the summer came quickly, and we had finished our part of the painting. We were pretty proud of it, but then at the end we noticed that they had hired some professional painters with spray guns that re-painted everything we had done in just a few days. Apparently, we'd spent six weeks only painting with primer paint for the initial coat. I guess the goal of the program was just to give us something to do instead of getting into trouble on the streets, but I still thought we did a pretty good job using only brushes.

CHAPTER 19

SPORTING SOPHOMORE

Intramural Basketball Champions—Quigley 1974

Sophomore year came, and I was still the same scrawny, seventy five pound freshman I had been as I entered my second year in high school. I decided that I was going to work out and play as much sports as possible so that I would get bigger.

Sports had become a big part of my life. Whether it was following the four major sports leagues on TV, playing around the neighborhood, or experiencing every sporting activity I could at Quigley, I was hooked. Even though I was small, my speed and coordination improved so that I could play most of the sports that were popular. I also started attending the unofficial weightlifting club after school, thinking I could quickly bulk up lifting weights.

The Quigley weight room next to the gym was only about the size of a large closet. I started just hanging around for a few days and quickly found out that there were only one or two people that attended on a regular basis, which I was happy about. I was worried about people making fun of me, so I was glad that not many students would actually see me in the weightlifting area.

The one upper-class student that was always there was a weightlifting junkie. He taught me all about how to lift weights with form and not just with power. Since I did not have a whole lot power, I listened closely and worked on my form. I started to lift heavier weights and even though it wasn't that much, I could hold my own, especially when you normalized it to my weight. That was always my go-to story with my friends: that, "pound for pound, I was stronger."

The fall of that year, my Uncle Father Callistus, who was the one who had sponsored my dad to come to the US, came to visit us in Chicago. It would be the first time that we would be reunited with one of our relatives from India in four years. My dad was very excited to see his brother again. He was on one of his missionary visits, so he stayed in a nearby parish for almost six weeks.

On the weekends, he would have my brothers and I come over to help him with his correspondence, which he had to make with all his constituents and donors for his many efforts back in India. Our job was to seal envelopes and place stamps. This was mind-numbing work, but we tolerated it because for lunch he would buy all of us Chicago's famous Polish sausages and fries from a nearby hot dog stand.

We also ended up meeting many of his American friends during his visit. I still remember spending that Thanksgiving with one of his friends in a southern suburb of Chicago. I ended up meeting my old sixth-grade math teacher from St. Boniface, Mrs. Joann, who was also at the get-together.

What I remember most about that afternoon is the Thanksgiving football match-up between The Cowboys and Redskins. An unknown quarterback for the Cowboys, named Clint Longley, had an unbelievable game.

Clint Longley, then a rookie, came into the game for injured Roger Staubach (who was the top quarterback in the league), with the Cowboys trailing 16-3 in the third quarter. They faced elimination from the playoffs if they didn't win that afternoon. After hitting Billy Joe Dupree for a thirty-five-yard touchdown pass, he led the Cowboys on a seventy-yard drive that ended in a touchdown run.

Finally, with the Cowboys behind 23-17 and with only seconds left with no time outs, Longley hit Drew Pearson for a fifty-yard Hail Mary pass, which gave the Cowboys a dramatic 24-23 come-from-behind victory. I always hated the Cowboys, and still do to this day, but that game was unbelievably exciting, and I started to watch and follow football much more closely.

During my sophomore year, I signed up for most intramural sports, including floor hockey, flag football, swimming, and basketball. All my street hockey background came in handy in floor hockey, and I captained my own team. We did well, though the competition was pretty weak in our league. Even in Chicago, not many kids played hockey. There were a couple of Quigley club ice hockey players in the league because it was in the off-season, and when we matched up against them it was a little more competitive.

I was definitely becoming a better athlete, but I was now the smallest kid in my class because the smallest kid during my freshman year overtook me. This really bummed me out for a few days, but I did get over it and continued to focus on my studies and sports.

Being the smallest kid in class did pose some challenges for my PE teacher during wrestling. For our final test in wrestling, I was eventually matched up with a kid named Steve, who was about twenty pounds heavier than me, but he was so uncoordinated that I was able to win my match easily.

One of the highlights of my sophomore year had to be the intramural basketball championships. I had been playing a lot of schoolground basketball and was starting to develop a decent shot. Our sophomore intramural team was actually good, mainly because we had Curtis, a great athlete in both baseball and basketball. I'm not sure how he got on the team, but I seem to remember that he may have been suspended out of the basketball team due to low grades, so he was eligible for the intramural teams.

During the regular season we did well and ended up in second place in the sophomore intramural league. I did okay, usually scoring one or two baskets a game. Curtis usually led every game in points, and he led us to victory on most days.

At the end of the intramural basketball season there was a single elimination tournament between the top four teams, and we clawed our way into the finals behind the scoring of Curtis and our team's overall defense and rebounding. We ended up playing the top team in the finals, and it was a game to remember for me. I ended up hitting my first jump-shot towards the end of the first quarter and, even though I didn't play that many minutes in the first half, I did end up contributing both on the offensive and defensive end.

I started on the floor in the second half, which built my confidence, and I played well. Most of the opposing team did not pay too much attention to me because of my size, but I was quick and ended up getting a couple of steals with one of them, ending in an easy lay-up for me on the offensive end.

The game was tight; right up to the last minute it was a low-scoring affair. Because of my play in the third quarter, I started the fourth quarter and I was so pumped I didn't have time to get nervous. I ended up hitting another jumper when Curtis found me open on the wing while the entire opposing team concentrated on our star player.

In the final minute of the game they were up on us by one, and I ended up with the ball; this time, instead of shooting I decided to go inside for a layup, since the right side of the court was wide open. I cut sharply to the right, but had two defenders close on me quickly, and I had to throw up a wild layup as I tried to duck under them, just like "Stormin' Norman" Van Lier of the Chicago Bulls.

The next thing I knew, I was on the floor. I fell on my shoulder, which was starting to hurt, but the pain quickly went away as soon as I heard the ref's whistle. He called a foul and directed me to the free throw line. Well, I ended up hitting both free throws, with the second one just barely rolling over the rim. It gave us the lead. I was ecstatic as my teammates, including Chris, who was one of my close friends at Quigley, started patting me on the way back to play defense for the final minute of play. No additional points were scored, and we ended up winning the championship game by one point.

The whole team celebrated as if we had just won the NBA World Championship title. All of us ended up getting a trophy, which was the first one I'd ever had, and I still display it proudly in my study to this day. My friend Chris told me right after the game that even though I only had eight points for the entire game, I was the leading scorer.

I tell my kids about this intramural championship game and how I was the leading scorer while holding my six-inch trophy high up in the air. I usually get a wide rolling of the eyes from both Matthew and Gina, but that doesn't stop me from telling the story over and over.

I finished up first semester of my sophomore year, and I felt my confidence growing. I had many friends both at school and in our neighborhood, and was feeling good about myself. Little did I know that around the corner my life was going to take another drastic turn.

Chapter 20

"RUN PEE WEE, RUN"

A more recent photo of our alley. We would have killed for the
paved, flat surface back in the day

It was now 1975, and this was the year that I really started getting into music. Hanging around my friend Gary, who played the guitar, I got introduced to albums and real rock 'n' roll. I asked my parents if they would buy me a guitar, but I was flatly denied. They didn't want me to get distracted from my studies. My dad also mentioned that they were expensive. I didn't push it with them and resorted to listening to AM radio stations that would play music.

One of my dad's colleagues from work, named Harry, came to visit one day. Apparently, he wanted to try Indian food, so my dad invited him to have dinner with us. My mom cooked a great Indian meal. The three of us were excited because my dad mentioned that Harry was one of the youngest employees that worked with him.

I don't remember his last name, but Harry had a cool beard, which was in fashion in the mid-seventies, and long hair. He and my dad must have also talked about music, because my dad played many of his favorite Indian songs, which Harry really enjoyed. My dad must have also mentioned my great interest for western music, because after dinner Harry mentioned he had something for me.

I wasn't exactly sure what he had in mind, but it turned out to be a moment that I would never forget. "Someone Saved My Life Tonight" by Elton John was a huge hit, and easily my favorite song that year when I was fifteen. The next thing I knew, my dad's friend gave me a brand-new copy of his album, *Captain Fantastic and the Brown Dirt Cowboy*, which included my favorite song. It was the very first album that I could call my own.

I was beyond ecstatic, and I asked my dad if he would play the album for us that night. My brothers and I listened to that album three or four times before my dad said enough was enough. I looked at the album closely that night with all its weird artwork. I wore out that album playing it over and over again over the years.

One of my favorite hobbies these days as an adult is to peruse second-hand vinyl record shops, and I recently found a mint copy of *Captain Fantastic and the Brown Dirt Cowboy* with all the original artwork included. I now have my very first album proudly displayed in my music room.

A few years ago, Suma and the kids and I were coming back from a day in Chicago downtown when we decided to go by my old neighborhood to see how things have changed. This time, both Gina and Matthew were excited to see their dad's old neighborhood, since Matthew was young the last time we went, and Gina was always ready for an adventure in the city.

I took the exit to head towards the west side of Chicago and we were in my old neighborhood again. How things change. The whole area looked different to me. The streets were all the same, but many of the homes had been refurbished and looked great. The old charm that I remembered was missing, but it certainly looked a lot nicer.

I went down the alley where I used to play as a kid and pointed out to Gina and Matthew that "This is where Dad, Uncle Jim, and Uncle Joe used to play hockey and football."

My son was laughing his head off, thinking about how narrow the alley was and wondering how we could play. I reminded him that we didn't have the facilities to play in like he does now, so instead the alley was our playground. Matthew played organized ice hockey in one of the suburban leagues from when he was eight until he was thirteen years old.

The backs of houses that faced the alley looked completely different: all modern and built up. As we were turning right from the alley to go to my old house, a female jogger dressed in trendy running clothes and a phone held up to her ear jogged past on the sidewalk.

The sight of this prompted me to comment, "Back when we were living here, if you saw someone running on the sidewalk, your antenna went up, because there could've been a gang chasing after them."

"Yeah, right Dad," Gina said incredulously.

We reached the front of our old house and I parked the car. I showed them the now-empty lot that was behind the main building, which was where our first apartment used to stand. As we pulled out from the street parking spot, I started telling them the story of when their uncles and I were being chased by a Chicago gang in the alley.

It was an early spring day, but we continued our hockey season in the neighborhood. It was nice not to wear a heavy jacket during hockey, because it was easier to stick-handle the puck on a sunny warm day. The alley was perfectly suited to play hockey in because the sides contained the puck, so we didn't have to go chasing after it if there was an errant pass. The only time we had to chase the puck was if somebody missed the net and it went into the street behind the net.

That day, there were eight kids playing, so we had four on a side, including the goalies. Because the alley was long, there was plenty of room to move around. I was having a good day. I was really starting to get good at playing street hockey after playing with all the neighborhood kids for the last five years. I also watched a lot of hockey and tried to emulate the Chicago Blackhawks stars of the day, like Stan Mikita and Bobby Hull.

Our team was winning, and I had already scored a couple of goals. A chubby kid named Rico was the goalie for the opposing team, and he was an easy target to beat. I would lift the puck with a wrist shot and he would usually turn his back, not wanting to get hit with it. In his defense, even the plastic pucks hurt if they hit you in the face.

My little brother Joseph, whom everyone in the neighborhood called "Pee Wee" because he was the youngest, was playing goal for my team. It was a nickname that stuck, and even to this day we still sometimes refer to him as "Pee Wee."

Even though he was small and the youngest, he was pretty athletic, and he was a good goalie. That day, he was on the end where our street was behind him. The game was going well, and I was about to shoot the puck back into the opposing zone when I heard their goalie, Rico, yell out, "It's a street gang, and they have guns."

Sure enough, as I looked behind him I did see several older kids on the other block, which was a good distance away from where we were playing, making a right turn into the alley and walking rapidly towards us. As I ran up near where Rico was and focused in on them, I could see that they all had on similar color clothing and it looked like they had something in their hands. Street gang activity had been increasing in our neighborhood, but I had never run across any of them before. I was not sure if it was a street gang or just a bunch of kids from further away wanting to give us a hard time, but Rico seemed convinced that the group approaching us were part of a gang.

I wasn't going to take any chances, so I told my friend Jimmy, the second-oldest, that we had all better go inside the house. He took a quick look down the street and didn't really like what he was seeing, so he turned and told me that we could all go to their house, which was right next to the alley. I really wanted to take my brothers to our house so that we could be with Mom and Dad.

As I was yelling out to my brother James that we needed to get out of there, I thought I saw the kids running towards us pointing something and making a shooting motion. I didn't hear anything that sounded like a gunshot, so I was not sure if they were just faking it.

"BBs," shouted Jimmy. "They have BB guns!" I told James to start running home, and I went by my little brother Joseph and helped him get out of his homemade goalie gear. We were near the intersection of the alley and the street we lived on, so it was just a quick dash to our house.

After I got him out of his gear, I could hear James yelling out, "Run, Pee Wee, run!"

I took my little brother's hand and we started running as fast as his feet could go. We reached the entrance of our house, where James was standing ready with the gate open for us. We all stepped in; I slammed the gate shut and bolted up the path leading to our front door.

My younger brothers James and Joseph in Chicago

173

As we got closer, I let go of my little brother's hand, stopped, and took a quick look back to see if they had made the turn from the alley to the street; no one was following. I'm sure they didn't want to come near the intersection, as they would be seen by others on the street. I was hoping all our friends had made it safely out.

We ran as fast as we could up the path without looking back and started frantically knocking at our front door. My mom opened the door and we stepped in. The three of us told her what had happened.

"There was a gang chasing us, and they had guns." I *did* clarify to my mom that they were BB guns, but all she heard were "guns."

There was a lot of discussion around the dinner table that night, recounting the story to our dad; he had been thinking about moving out to the suburbs. The East Village neighborhood had been in decline the last few years, and the BB gun incident solidified his decision to move. He was going to start looking for homes that he could afford in a nearby suburb of Chicago.

My brothers and I did not want to go. We said we would miss our friends and asked where we would go to school.

The idea stuck in my parent's heads, and nothing we said was going to change their minds. They had worked hard the past five years, saving up as much as they could by living frugally while providing for a family of five, but they knew the time was right. They had saved enough to cover the down payment needed for a modest suburban house, and with both of them working, they felt they could manage the mortgage payments. I didn't pay too much attention to the finances at the time.

After seeing a few homes over the next couple of months, they gave us an update that they had put in an offer for a home in a northwest suburb of Chicago. My dad went on to say that there were great public schools in the suburbs, and we would make new friends fast. He also said that we would have more room, both inside and outside the house.

My brothers still objected, but I went silent, thinking about a new neighborhood with bigger houses and meeting new people. It was strange that, although I would also miss all my friends and the city, I did look forward to the move. Even though I knew it would turn my world upside-down, I was ready for something new.

It was difficult to leave my friends, especially Gary and Jimmy, who were my two closest friends. Over those past five years they were the ones who knew me best, and the thought of making new friends just was not that appealing.

The offer on the house was accepted, and we were going to be homeowners in America. My parents were happy, but I had mixed feelings about leaving our home in Chicago.

I continued to attend Quigley North from our new home in Morton Grove, a Northwest suburb of Chicago. Even though I was still attending Quigley, it just wasn't the same as living in Chicago. I lived in Chicago proper for only five and a half years, but they were important ones for me, and I was going to miss living there. I was not too far away and would be able to visit the city frequently, but it was going to be different. I knew I would miss the neighborhoods, the city parks, and having people around me all the time.

Though I was sad to be leaving, I was also looking forward to the change. Just like my Uncle Father Callistus, who was the trailblazer that brought us to Chicago, and my parents, who took a big step to move away from their ancestral home and start over with three young kids in America, I never shied away from moving to new places, meeting different kinds of people, and pursuing interests that may not be in my comfort zone.

CHAPTER 21

GOODBYE CHICAGO

My Chicago

T he first semester of my junior year at Quigley was probably the most interesting for me because I was fully established with friends and I absolutely loved attending Quigley. But the travel back-and-forth from the suburbs was wearing on me. I was involved in a lot of activities, and taking the bus back home had become arduous. The winters were rough; waiting for the bus on the corner of Rush Street and Chicago Avenue that would take me to my new home was a cold affair. I usually tried to stand in the hotel lobby nearby. The hotel was situated on the corner, and most of the time the ushers let me stay.

If I somehow managed to scrounge some money, I always enjoyed having a quick cheeseburger and fries at the Jack in the Box across the street. After the Polish sausage, this was my next-favorite fast food.

My mom would always wonder how I was not hungry at dinnertime but as a teenager, now fully assimilated to American life and diet, Indian food just didn't taste as good anymore.

The classes at high school were getting tougher, since I was now taking more advanced classes like trigonometry and chemistry. The math and science classes continued to be my favorite. They were difficult, and I had to work hard to get good grades in both of those classes, but I liked the challenge.

My first chemistry class was exciting. I had a great teacher named Mr. Rozino and I was just mesmerized at the things I was learning. Even though I was more proficient at math, chemistry soon became my favorite subject. I didn't know it at the time, but Mr. Rozino's excitement about chemistry was infectious, and it was the springboard to one of my key areas of study in college and the rest of my career.

In college, I ended up studying Chemical Engineering, which gave me the opportunity to study further in the area of chemistry and math. This ultimately provided me a solid foundation for my career at Abbott Labs.

It was 2002, and I was well into my career at Abbott when it occurred to me that it had been twenty-five years since I graduated from high school. I hadn't been to any of my previous reunions, even though I received a few invitations; I just did not want to go.

As I pondered about the twenty-fifth anniversary of my Quigley class, a streak of nostalgia ripped through me as I was preparing for another meeting at work. I decided to look up Larry, one my buddies back at Quigley, whom I hadn't seen or even thought of in a long while.

I managed to track him down at his office across the Illinois border in Southern Wisconsin. I got his answering machine, so I left him a message telling him who I was, and if he knew whether there was going to be a twenty-five-year reunion. I was hoping he would remember me and call me back.

After grabbing something to eat at the Abbott cafeteria, I was walking back to my office when my assistant handed me a message that someone had just called. I was excited to see that it was Larry.

I called him back right away, and as soon as I heard that voice on the phone I knew it was Larry on the other end. It's funny how we always remember voices of our childhood friends, even decades later. I shut the door to my office and we excitedly exchanged greetings and brought each other up to date.

I got to business right away and asked him if there was going to be a twenty-five-year Quigley reunion. He told me that there had been a five year and a ten-year reunion, and he was disappointed that I had not been there. He mentioned that our school president, Dave, had organized the first two, but he hadn't heard anything as of yet.

Quigley was no longer a seminary or a boy's-only school. Quigley was a small school, so there was no organization that took up reunions; it had to be done by the alumni. Larry mentioned that there had been no fifteen-year or twenty-year reunion, so he just assumed that there was not going to be one. I told him to give me Dave's contact information so that I could inquire and persuade him for us to have a twenty-five-year reunion. We ran out of things to say on the phone, so we exchanged contact information and promised to keep in touch.

After I hung up with Larry, I thought about our twenty-five-year reunion and that we somehow had to get together to celebrate. Dave was not one of my close friends at Quigley, but I knew him well enough, so I was going to send him an e-mail to convince him that we needed to have a reunion. I wondered if he was even going to listen to me, since I had not graduated from Quigley.

You read correctly! I did not graduate from Quigley. When we moved from Chicago to the suburbs, I finished out my sophomore year and even finished my first semester of my junior year at Quigley. The bus rides were long, since I had to take two buses from Morton Grove to get to Quigley in downtown Chicago.

My last day at Quigley was tough. Our class size was down to around sixty, as the demerits had added up for many of the troublemakers, and they were ultimately kicked out. I was coming into my own at Quigley, but my relatives and friends convinced my parents that a fifteen-year-old shouldn't be riding the bus for three hours a day to go to high school. I was getting tired of all the traveling and was always a little tired by the time I got home from school. By the time I got all my homework done, I was exhausted. So I didn't put up too big of a fight.

I ended up finishing the second semester of my junior year and senior year at a suburban high school in Morton Grove. I absolutely hated my new high school, and my grades suffered. It was everything that Quigley wasn't. The new high school had thousands of kids versus the hundreds at Quigley. There were a few more Asian kids, but I was still the only Indian student that attended. The overall diversity of the student body was not anything like Quigley.

I also missed the family-type atmosphere that I experienced at Quigley. I was telling my wife one day, well into our marriage, that I couldn't even remember one student's name at the suburban high school, but I could list off about thirty names from my Quigley days. From the suburban high school, I could only think of rich, spoiled kids with cars.

My last day at Quigley was unceremonious: as it was before Christmas break, after completing my first semester of my junior year. Once again I was moving to a new school in the middle of a year, just like I had done in 5th grade. I said my goodbyes to my good friends Gary, Larry, and Chris, and I was on my way to high school in the Northwest suburbs. Other than Gary, whom I visited in Chicago a few more times, I eventually lost contact with all of my Quigley colleagues.

However, the Quigley Twenty-Fifth Year Reunion did end up happening, and I was right back to where I was when I met many of my classmates so long ago. I was part of the organizing committee, as my fellow colleagues welcomed me with open arms even though I did not graduate from Quigley.

Most of the graduating class showed up for the two days of festivities that took place at Quigley. We played basketball in our gym the night before and, to my surprise, I was able to score against some of the best basketball players that Quigley had to offer back in the day. It helped that I stayed in much better shape than many of my colleagues. It felt great to score some baskets in that old, green gym of ours.

After about forty-five minutes of playing, I did stop because unfortunately my legs cramped up so much that I couldn't play anymore. It happened on a play where I put a little too much effort into trying to block one of my taller classmate's shot. Old age catches up to all of us.

Two of our colleagues who became priests said mass in the Quigley chapel prior to the festivities. The chapel looked just as beautiful as it did twenty-five years earlier. It was strange seeing Tom up on the altar, as I can only remember how much of a wisecracking teenager he was during high school. I couldn't believe he became a priest. The other priest was Jerry, which did not surprise me as much.

Many of our wives were in the chapel with us, and they were shocked when, during the middle of the mass, all of us in unison yelled out a garbled "Bullshit" while coughing, just like we had done before to annoy the priests during our school years. All the wives were stunned at our inside joke, but I could see that the two priests were smiling as they went on with the mass as if nothing out of the ordinary had happened.

The evening of events was wonderful; it was as if we hadn't skipped a beat as we caught each other up in our lives and recalled all of the events that everyone seemed to remember. A few of the faculty, including Mr. McGreal (who was my favorite teacher) and Mr. Schaefer (our PE teacher) also showed up for the reunion.

I was so happy that my fellow colleagues let me join in on the celebrations. Our class president, Dave, even called me out in his opening remarks. "It took George Maliekal, who didn't even graduate with our class, to get us back together on our twenty-fifth anniversary. We are grateful to George for getting us back together again."

I kept thinking that it was I who was most grateful of all because I had a chance to come back to that magical place in downtown Chicago. I was able to meet all my old classmates who I had grown up with and helped me to establish my roots in the city I came to love. Since that night I've gone to subsequent reunions, and I can't wait to see my Quigley classmates again in a few years.

AFTERWORD

Eyes on the road ahead

I recently turned sixty, and a few years ago had the good fortune of retiring at a relatively young age from the only company I ever worked for after college. I worked for Abbott, a drug and medical device company, for thirty-four years. I was always proud to have worked for a Chicago-based company. It had its roots in the Ravenswood neighborhood, where Dr. Abbott ran a pharmacy. Ultimately, it became the global company, Abbott.

My career at Abbott was a fruitful one, with many intellectual challenges and the opportunity to work closely with some brilliant scientific and business colleagues. Together we made significant contributions to improving healthcare, and I am proud to have played a small part. A few of them became my good friends, and we continue to meet socially whenever we can. My varying roles at Abbott also allowed me to travel the world and meet some terrific individuals around the globe.

Early retirement has given me the luxury to truly enjoy and absorb life while giving back to our community: a community that accepted me when our family emigrated from India. After living a productive and busy early adulthood with college, family, career, and self-growth, I am now pursuing things that I only dreamed about doing when I was young: playing the guitar, mentoring college students, tutoring kids in math, enjoying the incredible sights that our world has to offer, and writing this book about my youth and all the individuals that helped shape my life.

When I was younger, I was focused on the task at hand; I didn't always take the time to really listen to what people had to say. Now, I have committed myself to being present, and to enjoy and engage with everyone in the moment.

My conversations with people used to be short and to the point as I focused on getting results and moving to the next step. I've always been logical and analytical, because that gave me the most efficient results. Retirement has given me the time to really put the other side of my brain to use and pursue interests that are totally different from what I did when I was younger. Now I take more time in trying to listen to what people have to say.

After sixty years, I have also learned to enjoy the moment and take life as it comes. It's amazing how much easier it is when you accept life as it is, and take the individuals that are always with you (and the new ones that you meet every day) as they are. In my younger years, I couldn't wait to see what was around the bend and get there quickly. I'm still always looking around the next bend, seeking out another adventure or some other new pursuit that I want to start, but now I savor the moment and take my time getting there, absorbing it all and truly enjoying it. I'm at a place where I am living my life as who I really am and not wearing the masks that we occasionally don in our daily lives.

I've also been able to spend more time with my family, especially with my wonderful wife Suma, who I am humbled to have by my side. Without a doubt, having her in my life has been the best thing that's ever happened to me. I have never met someone with so much energy seven days a week. Once she has a goal in mind, it's best to stay out of her way, because she won't stop until it's done—and she usually does it with a smile.

She is a wonderful role model for our kids, and we make a great team. She was extremely supportive of my busy career, with numerous days away from home that meant she did all the heavy-lifting back home to raise our two children while putting her own career on hold. She is now more active in her career and continues to support all my post-retirement pursuits.

I feel extremely comfortable in my own skin and even though it took a while, I'm here. I watch a lot of baseball these days with the Chicago White Sox doing well. It's a well-known fact that the curve ball in baseball (or cricket, for that matter) is the toughest pitch to hit for young hitters, and only after experiencing many of these and making adjustments do they master a curve ball and experience success. I had a number of curve balls thrown at me during my life, but ultimately figured out how to adjust to them, learn, and continue to march on. I truly believe facing those curve balls earlier in my life prepared me for facing the bigger challenges of life as an adult.

Retirement has also given me time to reflect on my life and realize that I didn't do it all by myself. These days, I hear the echoes of my ancestors and the individuals I met during those early years of my life frequently as I fully realize the impact they had on my life. I am extremely grateful for their care and the guidance they gave me. As I look back on all the events that took place in my life, and the people I met and interacted with throughout, there is nothing I regret. If I had the opportunity to live my life again, I would do it exactly the same way in a heartbeat. I would want nothing changed because every event, every personal interaction, and every thought I experienced is who I am.

If there's one piece of advice that I would give my younger self, it would be not to worry so much. Things always do get better the next morning, and in most cases one bad event or one failure does not define the person you are or will become. It is interesting that I don't even remember most of the things I worried about when I was young that kept me up at nights.

There were a lot of things that I did well to plan for my future when I was young, but if it weren't for my parents, my mentors, and my extended family, I would never be where I am now.

Finally, some of the things happening in our world lately keep me up at night. My awareness and anxiety level about these issues have risen as I get older. Like every parent, I worry about the type of world my kids, and hopefully grandkids, will grow old into.

As I write this, we are currently in the middle of the COVID-19 worldwide pandemic. The pandemic and its aftermath have further polarized our society. With access to information being a thousand times greater than when I was younger, gun violence, hate groups, religious wars in the name of God, and even greedy politics are in our faces twenty-four hours a day. The level of hate and violence that is exhibited, and then blown out of proportion in the media, is not how most everyday citizens wish to live.

Every generation has dealt with these forces and had to navigate through them. I know we will also. Therefore, my belief is with humanity and everyday citizens empowering themselves to make meaningful change for continued progress. It's with moms and dads like mine, nurturing the next generation of Earth's caretakers. It's with individuals like my teachers, mentors, colleagues, and friends who made my life richer by never giving up on encouraging me to grow and succeed. It's with my kids, along with many other youngsters, who will be taking the mantle from my generation. Based on the creativity, smarts, and compassion I see in the younger generation, I'm convinced that they will be even more productive in all aspects of life than we are currently.

It's also with me for the remainder of my life to make a difference. I was taught to learn and judge right from wrong in my youth, which I tested and refined through my life experiences, and I am now committed to continue caring about the Earth and its inhabitants.

I'm not sure how long I'm destined for this world, but I hope one day I'll get to personally give to my grandchildren a copy of this book so that they can get a glimpse into how their family made their way from Southern India to the US, prospered, and continue to contribute to our collective community.

As I write these closing words, it's comforting to know that my own children, Gina and Matthew—whom I can't convey in words how happy they make me feel each time I see them—will have my childhood story in my own words that they can one day pass on to their children and grandchildren. Hopefully, it inspires them to write their own stories to pass down, so that future generations can experience important parts of their journey.

My journey on Earth so far has been wonderful, and as I look to the future with my wife and partner in crime by my side, I feel more alive than ever. The fire in my heart is still burning hot, and the light in my eye is still shining as brightly as ever as I continue to head down my path with a smile on my face, knowing I still have a long way to go.

I recently had a chat on Facebook with a few of my Quigley North high school classmates. The ensuing discussion was with three of my favorite people from Quigley: Gary Sylvie, my Big Brother Ed, and our history teacher, Mr. McGreal. The comments centered on how times have changed and how we just can't do the feats we were able to do when we were younger, which was when Mr. McGreal interjected, "Keep your eyes on the road ahead, gentlemen."

Fifty years later, my high school teacher's comments still ring true for me. My past is worth remembering and documenting, but my eyes need to be keenly focused on the road ahead: as they will while I head out once again to experience the world.

Chicago's oldest symbol, still in use today

ACKNOWLEDGEMENTS

Writing my first book about my youth was harder than I thought it would be, but it was much more rewarding than I could ever have imagined. I want to first thank my loving wife, Suma, for all her support throughout the process, including the multiple readings of drafts, checking on accuracy of statements, and the beautiful oil painting she made of my beloved Chicago skyline, which we used for the book cover. It was truly a team effort, Suma.

I also want to thank my two children, Gina and Matthew, for all their encouragement and listening to Dad endlessly talk about his book. A special thanks to Gina, who with her keen insights assisted me in bringing several of the stories to life through her careful edits of the early drafts.

Writing a book about one's youth is a surreal process. Many individuals, including my mom, brothers, uncle, aunts, friends, classmates, and teachers who were a part of my story helped me to distill my thoughts, confirm my memories, and make this book a reality. A very special thanks goes out to my good friend Betty Mohr, an author and playwright who was my boss at Marshall Field's during my college years. She continually encouraged and inspired me to keep writing, even when I had doubts about finishing this book.

Finally, to the team at Cascadia Author Services, who helped me independently publish this book, including Heidi, Marla, and especially Michelle for walking me diligently and patiently thorough every step of the process.

Thank You All

CPSIA information can be obtained
at www.ICGtesting.com
Printed in the USA
BVHW010648160721
611837BV00039B/950/J